ADVANCES IN LIFELONG EDUCATION

LIFELONG EDUCATION
AND
EVALUATION PRACTICE

A Study on the Development of a Framework
for Designing Evaluation Systems at the School
Stage in the Perspective of Lifelong Education

LIFELONG EDUCATION
AND
EVALUATION PRACTICE

A Study on the Development of a Framework
for Designing Evaluation Systems at the School
Stage in the Perspective of Lifelong Education

by

RODNEY SKAGER
University of California, Los Angeles

UNESCO INSTITUTE FOR EDUCATION, HAMBURG
and
PERGAMON PRESS
OXFORD · NEW YORK · TORONTO · SYDNEY · PARIS · FRANKFURT

U.K.	Pergamon Press Ltd., Headington Hill Hall, Oxford OX3 0BW, England
U.S.A.	Pergamon Press Inc., Maxwell House, Fairview Park, Elmsford, New York 10523, U.S.A.
CANADA	Pergamon of Canada Ltd., 75 The East Mall, Toronto, Ontario, Canada
AUSTRALIA	Pergamon Press (Aust.) Pty. Ltd., 19a Boundary Street, Rushcutters Bay, N.S.W. 2011, Australia
FRANCE	Pergamon Press SARL, 24 rue des Ecoles, 75240 Paris, Cedex 05, France
FEDERAL REPUBLIC OF GERMANY	Pergamon Press GmbH, 6242 Kronberg-Taunus, Pferdstrasse 1, Federal Republic of Germany

First edition 1978

British Library Cataloguing in Publication Data
Skager, Rodney
Lifelong education and evaluation practice.
- (Advance studies in lifelong education; vol. 4).
1. Continuing education - Evaluation
I. Title II. Unesco. Institute for Education
III. Series
374   LC5219   78-40003
ISBN 0-08-021812-1 Hardcover (Pergamon)
ISBN 0-08-021813-X Flexicover (Pergamon)
ISBN 92-820-1013 9 Hardcover (UIE)
ISBN 92-820-1014 7 Flexicover (UIE)

In order to make this volume available as economically and as rapidly as possible the author's typescript has been reproduced in its original form. This method unfortunately has its typographical limitations but it is hoped that they in no way distract the reader.

"The UNESCO Institute for Education, Hamburg, is a legally independent entity. While the programmes of the Institute are established along the lines laid down by the General Conference of UNESCO, the publications of the Institute are issued under its sole responsibility; UNESCO is not responsible for their content.
   The points of view, selection of facts and opinions expressed are those of the author and do not necessarily coincide with official positions of the UNESCO Institute for Education, Hamburg."

The designations employed and the presentation of the material in this publication do not imply the expression of any opinion whatsoever on the part of the UNESCO Secretariat concerning the legal status of any country or territory, or of its authorities, or concerning the delimitations of the frontiers of any country or territory.

*Printed in Great Britain by William Clowes & Sons Limited
London, Beccles and Colchester*

ABOUT THE AUTHOR

SKAGER, Rodney (United States). Is an Associate Professor in the Graduate School of Education at the University of California, Los Angeles. He has broad experience in the field of educational evaluation and in the disciplines of measurement and educational research methods. For the past ten years Professor Skager has also been associated with the Center for the Study of Evaluation at UCLA. Before joining the faculty of the School he was a research psychologist with the Educational Testing Service in Princeton, New Jersey, and later with the America College Testing Program in Iowa City, Iowa. While on academic leave during 1975-1976 he served as Senior Educational Research Specialist at the UNESCO Institute for Education in Hamburg.

CONTENTS

43410

x   Contents

FOREWORD

For several years now Unesco has formulated its educational programs and policies around the concept of lifelong education. Consistent with this emphasis, the Governing Board of the Unesco Institute for Education in 1972 decided that the Institute develop and carry out a long-term research program designed to elaborate and concretize the concept of lifelong education. In this activity, the Governing Board recommended that the program be concentrated on the substantive aspects of school level education.

At the time the resulting program was initiated it was evident that a great deal of thinking had already been done on lifelong education. Much room existed, however, for the clarification and systematization of its conceptual features and operational principles. Likewise, the need for coming to grips with the concrete implications of the concept became apparent especially in relation to the curriculum, the teaching and learning process, the educational staff, and the criteria and procedures by which evaluation might be conducted.

The initial phase of this work consisted of a series of conceptual studies on the characteristics and implications of lifelong education as well as on the interdisciplinary foundations of lifelong education. The outcomes of these efforts have been widely disseminated among Member States of UNESCO, national centers for educational research and development, professional groups, and individual scholars. The work reported here is firmly grounded on this earlier conceptual work, and is also in many ways a parallel project with a recently completed multi-national study into the development of criteria and procedures for the evaluation of school curricula under lifelong education. The author of the present monograph collaborated closely in that project which was in a number of respects an initial attempt to concretize the principles of lifelong education through their application to curriculum evaluation.

Application to evaluation is perhaps one of the most effective ways to render abstract educational principles more concrete. In order to evaluate, it is necessary to be able to recognize educational principles as they actually influence activities in schools and other formal and informal structures for the delivery of education. However, the present monograph is also a conceptual document. It seeks to explore what evaluation would be like under lifelong education and to derive a set of rules under which it would operate. It also points up the significant areas where further research and development will be required for maximizing the usefulness and constructive character of evaluation for lifelong education. It is therefore especially intended to serve as a stimulus for further work.

The Unesco Institute for Education was fortunate to have the assistance of Professor Rodney Skager in carrying out this project. In addition to his knowledge and experience in the field of measurement and educational research, Professor Skager's professional qualifications include a 10 year association with the Center for the Study of Evaluation at the University of California, Los Angeles, where he served as Program Director. I am confident that his monograph will be widely accepted as a significant extension of the work that has already gone on at the Institute.

M. Dino Carelli
Director

ACKNOWLEDGEMENTS

I wish to express special appreciation to all those who
gave so freely of their time by participating in the meeting of
project consultants which convened at the Unesco Institute in
Hamburg, May 10-14, 1976. The regular members of the panel consisted of Professor L.B. Daniels of the University of British
Columbia, Professor Abraham Magendzo of the Universidad Catoli-
ca de Chile, Prof. Dr. Christoph Wulf, Comprehensive University
of Siegen, FRG, and recently of the Deutsches Institut für Inter-
nationale Pädagogische Forschung, Mr. Péter Inkei of the Educational Research Institute of the Hungarian Academy of Sciences,
Dr. Chew Tow Yow of the Curriculum Development Centre of the
Malaysian Ministry of Education, and my own colleague, Professor Richard Shavelson of the University of California, Los Angeles. In addition, Professor T.N. Postlethwaite of the University of Hamburg and recently of the International Institute for
Educational Planning (Unesco), was able to attend most of the
meetings of the panel. All of these individuals along with
others mentioned below contributed valuable suggestions toward
the improvement of the original manuscript for this report. The
work is significantly better as a result of their powers of
thought and persuasion, and doubtless would have been better
yet had I been able to incorporate all of the useful suggestions that were made.

Individuals who made helpful independent comments on sec-
tions of the first draft of the manuscript included Dr. R.H.
Dave of the International Institute for Educational Planning
(Unesco) and formerly of the Unesco Institute in Hamburg, Dean
John I. Goodlad of the Graduate School of Education at UCLA,
Dr. Douglas Pidgeon, Director, Initial Teaching Alphabet Foun-
dation, and Dr. Ruth Wong, then Director of the Institute of
Education, Republic of Singapore.

I must express my equally sincere appreciation for the
help and support extended by colleagues at the Unesco Institute

for Education during the 13 months that I was privileged to be a member of the staff. These include Professor Arthur Cropley, on leave from the University of Regina, Dr. Otto Mihály, on leave from the Educational Research Institute of the Hungarian Academy of Sciences, as well as Mr. Kenneth Robinson and Mr. Peter Sachsenmeier, regular staff members of the Unesco Institute.

I am especially grateful to Dr. M. Dino Carelli, Director of the Unesco Institute for Education, for making it possible for me to spend a rewarding year at work on this and other projects of the Institute and for his frequent and thoughtful support and encouragement.

Finally, my appreciation is also extended to Mrs. Louise Silz whose rapid, accurate, and often more than reproductive work on the manuscript provided an example that helped me to work much faster than I might otherwise have done.

Rodney Skager
Hamburg, 1976

CHAPTER 1

EVALUATION AND THE PRINCIPLES OF LIFELONG EDUCATION

Evaluation and Educational Change

"Evaluation" as a term in the ordinary language refers to processes that are an integral part of the daily lives of individuals in all societies. Whatever may be its particular form or purpose, the act of evaluation implies (a) an initial experience or "finding-out" that is (b) interpreted by means of standards, rules, or principles in order to (c) arrive at a judgment of goodness or desirability. When described in these general terms, evaluation is readily seen as a fundamental regulating mechanism in the lives of men and women in all societies. It is a means by which individuals and groups constantly interpret their own experience for the purpose of shaping future experience. It is not surprising that the generalized skill or capacity of evaluation was assigned by Bloom (1956) and his collaborators to the highest level in the hierarchy of cognitive functions.

Educational evaluation is usually associated with growth, innovation, and development. It may focus on the needs and progress of learners themselves in order to facilitate decisions affecting those learners directly. Alternatively, evaluation may assess the overall effectiveness and desirability of the conditions that affect learning in a given context. Whether focused on the learner or on the conditions that influence learning, evaluation is the means by which participants in the learning/teaching process as well as concerned outsiders find out whether or not changes are needed, guide the development of means for dealing with those needs, and determine the overall effectiveness of the solutions that have evolved.

Much evaluation in education is informal, impressionistic and immediate. It is based on the personal judgments of learners, teachers and others directly involved in the learning process. While more systematic and formal approaches to evaluation will be stressed here, the role of the informal or qualitative is recognized and respected. Both approaches are necessary. Without them the only basis for changing the status quo would be a mindless policy of change for its own sake. Informed and intelligent attempts at change and modernization of the educational systems of any society are inevitably dependent on evaluation.

Havelock (1971) and Huberman (1973) emphasized the relationship between innovation and evaluation in their descriptions of three basic models for educational change. Each model incorporates one or more evaluation components. The first, or *research and development model*, devolves from the familiar cycle of (a) basic research leading to discovery, (b) design and engineering of applications, (c) diffusion, and (d) adoption by potential users. This particular model assigns a role to evaluation at the design and engineering phase, usually referred to as "formative" evaluation, and at the final or "summative" phase of adoption. The second, or *social interaction model*, stresses the interpersonal, leadership, and organizational aspects of diffusing innovation. A central role is assigned to communication and persuasion. Two of the five steps in the model are evaluative. The first of these involves a "trial in the mind of the user", presumably based on information about the potential innovation. If this information (in itself derived in part from earlier evaluations) is convincing in terms of the context in which the potential user must operate, the change or innovation can be evaluated more formally through actual use on a trial basis. The third, or *problem-solving model*, has its analogue in clinical practice. It involves (a) diagnosis of the needs implied in a recognized problem situation, (b) participation of an outside "change-agent" who acts in the role of a non-directive counselor or advisor, and (c) active participation on the part of the user in seeking solutions, especially those which utilize already existing internal resources. The strong motivational base that accompanies self-initiated change is emphasized in this model. Evaluation enters in the diagnosis of the "problem" and in the weighing of possible "solutions". It also occurs at the summative stage when one or more of the solutions is put into operation.

The models described by Huberman refer primarily to situations where large numbers of learners are exposed to innovations in instructional materials, teaching styles, organization-

al contexts, or modes of learning. The models nevertheless
have their analogues in the evaluation of learners in the classroom or other learning situation. For example, teachers use
their own version of the social interaction model by enhancing
the motivation of their students through leadership and persuasion. Teachers likewise use the problem-solving model when
acting as counselors helping learners to diagnose and deal with
their own problems. Even the research and development model
has its own counterpart in the informal process by which teachers and others develop hypotheses about learners and test them
out through trial and error. Each of these classroom analogues
to the educational change models has its own internalized evaluation components.

Evaluation is so naturally embedded in any educational activity that one does not have to argue for its importance.
Rather, the real concern is that evaluation be conducted in a
manner that is as useful and constructive as possible. Evaluation must be adaptive to the values and educational philosophies
of the participants in a given educational process. Lifelong
education, as described below, suggests certain preferred modes,
foci, and functions for evaluation. The purpose of this monograph is to clarify what these are and then to derive guide-
lines for the development of evaluation practice within the
perspective of lifelong education.

Social and Cultural Contexts for Lifelong Education

Lifelong education is described as a "master concept for
educational policies" in the 1972 Unesco report of the International Commission chaired by Edgar Faure. Strictly speaking,
however, lifelong education is not a concept or theory, but a
set of basic principles through which the Commission, its spon-
soring agency, and its growing ranks of supporters hope to stimulate worldwide educational reform over the coming decades.

The principles of lifelong education reflect contemporary
social forces. In the more highly developed countries rapid
changes in technology are generating new patterns of productive
activity. At the same time, less developed countries are strug-
gling to catch up educationally and technologically. Although
the educational needs of more and less developed societies are
different in many respects, there are still significant areas
of communality. Major adaptations in work-skills, attitudes,
and responsibilities must be made within the productive lifetimes of individual citizens in both types of societies. Vir-

tually all contemporary societies, even those just beginning to experience rapid technological development, already utilize a variety of educational structures to help citizens cope with changes in patterns of work and life style. The institutional means for facilitating this process are certainly not confined to "schooling" nor to the period of life that has in the past been assigned to schooling. The need for a citizenry "educable" throughout life is widely appreciated. In order to adapt, mature individuals must be willing and able to engage in systematic learning. In this sense, at least, more and less developed societies are on common ground.

Many less developed nations are finding it impossible to build up schooling on traditional patterns fast enough to maintain their projected rates of economic growth. This is true in spite of the fact that such countries have in many cases increased the proportion of their gross national product spent on schooling faster that the GNP itself has increased (Faure, et al., 1972). Formal schooling in underdeveloped countries is also often criticized for being responsible for the growth of urbanized elites neither willing nor able to participate in the development of rural areas. As a result there is great interest in identifying and developing alternative methods for delivering education - methods that are less expensive and better integrated with the communities where target populations reside, but which are also co-ordinated wherever possible with formal schooling.

Highly developed societies also look to alternative educational delivery systems, though for partly different reasons. Increasingly schools are seen as an element in a larger educational network aimed at fostering new work-skills in citizens past school age, and at enhancing the productive and satisfying use of free time. Not only must people learn new skills relating to work (Husén, 1968), they also require means to deal constructively and even creatively with the free time that is available in many highly developed societies. The danger to the individual and to the larger society of passivity and inactivity in the face of more and more leisure is apparent. Education becomes the primary social tool for promoting individual growth and self-realization (Dave, 1973 and Lengrand, 1970). This particular need is considerably less significant in societies where a daily struggle for survival is a reality for many citizens.

At least one other factor operating in both more and less

developed countries has had an important influence on the principles of lifelong education. Attempts to reduce or eliminate
social inequalities in many societies have leaned heavily on
education. Institutions that were once pillars of elitist social systems are now pressed into the service of egalitarianism.
Whatever the ideological origin of the press for change, a faith
in the power of education to promote various types of equality
is apparent in many if not all national societies.

Lifelong education is not merely an invention of educational theorists and visionaries. Its principles summarize changes
in the functions of education that have been apparent for some
time and in many places. In this sense lifelong education is
not an original idea nor does it refer to some single idealized,
total educational program. Rather, its manifestations reflect
broad, qualitative principles that take different concrete forms
in different societies. Lifelong education cannot be judged as
an integrated educational philosophy or theory. It is simply a
way of conceptualizing and communicating what are in fact worldwide trends towards the enhancement and variegation of education's role in society.

Defining Lifelong Education

The set of twenty-one principles of lifelong education
proposed by Faure et al., (1972) are eclectic and inclusive.
They are also grounded on egalitarian values. The principles
define ultimate ends, but avoid being prescriptive about means.
Taken together, they present a holistic view of education operating within an idealized "learning society" - a society in
which individuals engage in personally and socially meaningful
learning throughout their lives and in which the means of learning are distributed by various institutions and made equally
available to all.

The consistent emphasis on equality and democratization
that is manifest in writings on lifelong education is especially
significant for evaluation. In the pertinent literature evaluation is held to be a vital function, but one which in the past
has often functioned to promote and maintain social elitism and
unwholesome competition among learners (Council of Europe, 1972).
Giving the learner individually and collectively more control
over the learning process would help to develop autonomy and
co-operative interdependence. The development of self-evaluation skills in learners is seen as highly desirable. So, too,
are flexible and non-punitive approaches to evaluation as ap-

plied to the learner (Schwartz, 1970).

Inclusiveness of Principles of Lifelong Education

The original principles of lifelong education have been extensively elaborated since the publication of the Faure report. Dave (1973, 1975) derived a set of "concept characteristics" and applied them to topics such as school curriculum, learning strategies, and evaluation. This work will not be summarized here, except where it is especially pertinent to evaluation. However, Dave's 1975 report does emphasize the scope and inclusiveness of the principles.

> "Lifelong education is a comprehensive concept which includes formal, non-formal and informal learning extended throughout the life-span of an individual to attain the fullest possible development in personal, social and professional life. It seeks to view education in its totality and includes learning that occurs in the home, school, community, and workplace, and through mass media and other situations and structures for acquiring and enhancing enlightenment".
> (Dave, 1975, p.43)

Dave's interpretation of lifelong education stresses the connection between learning and the highest levels of human development. Education is the primary vehicle for personal and collective growth. Evaluation under this sort of conception of the social function of education would have to move beyond the assessment of attainment and into the assessment of capacity for future attainment. A unifying theme for evaluation is the concept of "educability" and the ways in which it might be enhanced in learners.

While the above might seem unduly idealistic to some, there is also a highly pragmatic basis for formulating lifelong education in such inclusive terms. The member states of Unesco cover the full spectrum of development and incorporate all national political and social systems. The educational program of the organization cannot be other than inclusive. Whatever principles are incorporated in the program should be flexible enough to be interpretable in terms of the needs of virtually any society. Thus, it has already been noted that non-formal educational means are pertinent to the needs of both developed and developing nations, but for mainly different purposes and undoubtedly in different forms.

In a similar manner, lifelong education leaves room for the full spectrum of progressive educational thought and practice. Many of the criticisms and proposals of the "deschooling" movement have found a place, yet schooling itself is retained. Likewise there is a place for both pragmatists and humanists, as well as for all aspects of educational technology (Faure, et al., 1972).

Evaluation Criteria for Lifelong Education

Evaluation criteria are standards against which phenomena may be judged and appraised. Strictly speaking, criteria as standards ordinarily define regions along some descriptive dimension distinguishing what is desirable from what is undesirable. Criteria are thus concrete referents for abstract principles or rules defining what is good. Examining whatever evaluation criteria have been proposed is therefore a useful way to identify the values and assumptions which underlie educational movements.

Work on specifying evaluative criteria for lifelong education is still in an early stage. However, a start in this process was made in a multi-national curriculum evaluation project coordinated by the Unesco Institute for Education. One of the two major goals of the project was to isolate the salient characteristics of curricula incorporating the principles of lifelong education. National teams from Japan, Romania, and Sweden, all nations with centralized curriculum planning, met in joint session initially to arrive at a first list of criteria. This list was later modified extensively by each team working in its own national setting, and the resulting criteria were used in a variety of national curriculum evaluation studies. Finally, the teams met again to compare results and to develop a combined or multi-national list. A report by Skager and Dave (1977) summarizes the procedures and implications of the project as a whole.

The combined criterion list is ordered into three levels of specificity. At the most general level there are five clusters or categories which represent basic principles of lifelong education. Each of the clusters in turn is divided into still relatively general criteria defining desirable states and conditions. Finally, at a third level two or more "specifications" were developed for each criterion statement. In some cases the specifications are simply elaborations of the criterion statement and in other cases they refer to applications or illustra-

tions. It should be pointed out that this work is regarded by
its authors as no more than a starting point. Even the specifications are relatively general in nature and allow for more
specific interpretation within the context of a particular society. Indeed, the national lists were in two of the three cases
considerably more specific than the combined, multi-national
list.

The criteria from the final report are reproduced and elaborated below. Each criterion statement is accompanied by a
single specification by way of illustration. Many (though by
no means all) of the statements reflect the fact that the project focused on curriculum evaluation. These statements tend
to refer to activities generated by the school or other educational agents rather than to outcomes evident in the learner
or in the society. However, the latter can in many cases be
inferred from statements about the nature of the curriculum.
The following list should help to clarify the basic principles
of lifelong education.

I.   HORIZONTAL INTEGRATION: Functional integration of all
     social agencies fulfilling educational functions, of
     elements of the curriculum at any given level, and
     among learners with different personal characteristics.

The first criterion cluster stresses relationships between
schools and all other social institutions and structures that
fulfil an educational function. This principle reflects the
dissatisfaction expressed by writers such as Husén (1974) and
Richmond (1975) with the common tendency to identify education
in general with the particular institution of schooling. It
also reflects skepticism, partly based on research findings,
concerning the relative influence of schooling as a determinant
of educational outcomes in contrast to factors that are not
associated with the school (Averch, et al., 1972). Arguments
for developing educational resources outside of formal schooling lie at the foundation of the entire framework of lifelong
education (Richmond, 1975).

"The idea of learning outside of the school raises two
major issues in any future theory and practice of education. The first of these is the one which is commonly referred to as 'lifelong learning'. The other
concerns the as yet largely unexplored domain of informal learning - in the home, at the work place, in
community life - in which the normal teacher-pupil relationship does not apply". (Richmond, p.8)

Criteria and Illustrative Specification

1. Integration between school and home

   School and home maintain complementary roles in education of the child.

2. Integration between school and community (local, national, international)

   Community facilities, resources and experience are used for school activities.

3. Integration between school and world of work

   School activities are related to actual production through study visits and trainee periods at different places of work.

4. Integration between school and cultural institutions, organizations and activities

   Films, theatre, music, museums, libraries and sport are incorporated in the school curriculum.

5. Integration between school and mass media

   Ability is developed in learners to evaluate critically information presented via mass media.

6. Integration of subjects of study

   Different school subjects are integrated into wider fields of study.

7. Integration between curricula subjects and extra-curricular activities

   Learners acquire skills for use in leisure.

8. Integration of learners having different characteristics

   Students of different ethnic, physical, intellectual, religious, and social characteristics jointly participate in the learning process.

None of the specifications of horizontal integration are original, and in fact are undoubtedly already utilized to some degree in many, if not most, countries. Considered together, however, they illustrate how seemingly isolated practices are

in reality representative of broader, programmatic principles
incorporated in the lifelong education framework. Other criteria could be included, of course. Personality integration
has been suggested by some, but elements of this complex principle are more at home in the third and fourth clusters which
summarize desirable characteristics in learners.

II.   VERTICAL ARTICULATION: Articulation among curriculum
      components at different levels of schooling and be-
      tween school curricula and pre- and post-school edu-
      cation.

The second cluster refers to another type of linkage, in
this case that connecting educational delivery systems typically
oriented to different age levels of the population. In the
literature on lifelong education pre- and post-schooling are
not merely supplementary to the school, but rather they stand
as equal partners. Theory and research on human development,
particularly findings pointing to the formative impact of early
childhood learning, are frequently cited in support of pre-
school education. The new knowledge and skills that adults must
acquire during their productive lifetimes likewise suggest increased utilization of post-school education. However, the main
emphasis here is not simply on the enhancement of educational
opportunity in the pre- and post-school years, but rather on
the establishment of temporal continuity in the learning process, both within and between levels.

Criteria and Illustrative Specifications

1. Integration between pre-school experiences and
   the school

   Interest in future school learning is awakened
   with visits to school and other extra curricular
   incentives.

2. Integration between different grades or other
   levels within the school

   Organization and study content at different
   school levels are linked systematically.

3. Integration between school and post-school activities

   Learners are informed about organization, operation and entrance requirements of different forms
   of adult education.

In evaluation it is often useful to distinguish between educational *means* and educational *ends*. For example, a particular mode of study such as learning by discovery could be seen as a means to at least two kinds of ends or goals. An immediate end might be mastery of some particular domain of educational content such as a mathematical relationship or a principle of physics. The second, longer term end, might be the development in the learner of a generalized competency for independent learning and discovery that is transferable to the mastery of other content domains.

Means and ends distinctions, however, are not always so easily made and often are quite artificial. Dewey observed that means are often constituents of ends and ends often "... usable as means to further ends". (Archambault, 1974, p.106). Thus the kinds of capacities that might be associated with the "educability" concept could be defined as ends in the sense of reference to developed capacities in the learner. But such capacities are equally means to other kinds of learning ends.

Likewise, it is often convenient to look upon educational methods or processes as means, while viewing outcomes manifested in learners (or in the society as a whole) as ends, as in the discovery learning example just given. But this distinction often breaks down as well. Equality of opportunity in the instructional process could be seen as a way of promoting certain kinds of desirable characteristics in learners, but equality as a principle may also be valued in its own right. It can stand as a criterion for evaluating an educational endeavour without regard to the kinds of outcomes that might be associated with its presence.

The two criterion lists just provided refer primarily to ways of structuring education rather than to outcomes associated with characteristics of learners or with changes in the larger society. In any case, how useful is it to attempt to specify "outcomes" of the various aspects of horizontal integration? Presumably when implemented these structural and organizational principles would contribute to the greater utilization of educational resources by people of virtually all ages. But many other factors would also be involved in promoting such utilization and the particular role of horizontally integrated structures would be difficult to separate out. While in one sense both of these clusters represent "means" for facilitating desirable changes in people and their societies, for practical purposes they might as well be viewed as defining ends in their

own right. Criteria in the two clusters point to structural
and organizational needs in education that appear to be desirable on both conceptual and pragmatic grounds.

Some of the other criteria in the clusters that follow also constitute what are usually thought of as means in the sense
that they refer to educational processes or structures rather
than to outcomes manifested in learners or in the society as a
whole. Since they are derived from the principles of lifelong
education they are likewise considered here as criteria in the
same sense that desired changes in learners are criteria. While
much of the attention of evaluation practice in recent years has
focused on outcomes, there is no reason why desired educational
processes, methods, or structural arrangements cannot be criteria in their own right as long as they embody principles that
are basic to a given conception of education.

III. ORIENTATION TO SELF-GROWTH: Development in learners
     of personal characteristics that contribute to a long-
     term process of growth and development including real-
     istic self-awareness, interest in the world and in
     other people, the desire to achieve, internalized cri-
     teria for making evaluations and judgments, and over-
     all integration of the personality.

This cluster incorporates criteria that define various aspects of personal growth as it has been stressed in recent hu-
manistic writings (Rogers, 1969). Several of the elements of
the broader concept of educability obviously originate here,
especially those relating to motivation in the learner. While
the criteria below might be biased in the sense of being phrased
in terms of the development of the individual rather than of
the larger society, they do have implications for the latter
since the society will reflect the characteristics of the people who make it up.

There is no denying the difficulties involved in defining
and attempting to measure the kinds of processes and characteristics listed below, to say nothing of the kinds of mistakes
that could be made in attempting to foster them. This does not
mean that such criteria can be ignored. MacDonald (1974) in
his recent critique of evaluation practice suggests in this
regard that,

   "The goals...are the crucial and significant aspect of
   the evaluation process, not the process of measuring.
   But as is often the case with men, our dreams outreach

our means, and what we are witnessing in education today is a wholesale miniaturizing of goals to satisfy the primitiveness of our measurement abilities. We have really gained very little and risked much if we allow our goals for schooling to be determined by our ability to measure". (p.3)

Criteria and Illustrative Specifications

1. Self-understanding

   Learners are aware of responsibility for own growth.

2. Interest in human beings and in environmental world

   Learners are interested in their physical and biological environment.

3. Achievement motivation

   Learners are motivated to improve their own abilities (cognitive, affective and psychomotor).

4. Establishment of internal judgment criteria

   Learners are able to formulate opinions independently.

5. Establishment of progressive values and attitudes

   Learners develop flexible thinking and tolerance.

6. Integration of personality

   Learners explore and assimilate an ideal model for personal development.

The concept of self-growth is obviously highly complex. It combines criteria relating to self-awareness, motivation, and affective orientation. The work that has been done so far, while incomplete, does sketch in the basic referents of this particular criterion cluster.

IV. SELF-DIRECTED LEARNING: Individualization of the learning experience toward the goal of developing the learner's own skills and competencies in the planning, execution and evaluation of learning ac-

tivities both as an individual and as a member of a
co-operative learning group.

The significance of self-direction in learners to lifelong
education has already been cited. The development of such autonomy in learners is simultaneously a means to an end and an end
in itself. The 14th principle of the Faure, et al. (1972) report suggests the importance attached to this criterion cluster:

"The new educational ethos makes the individual the
master and creator of his own cultural progress.
Self-learning, especially assisted self-learning,
has irreplaceable value in any educational system".
(p.209)

Virtually all of the papers on lifelong education abstracted in the Dave and Stiemerling (1973) monograph elaborate on at
least some aspects of this cluster by referring to generalized
skills and capacities not tied to particular educational content
and useful for later learning. These include language and communication skills, especially foreign languages, learning and
study skills including the organization of learning, social
skills contributing to group learning and problem-solving and
cognitive and thinking skills relating to observation and the
organization of experience and expression. Not all of these
skills appear on the list below, but they are at least implied
in the statements about curriculum. Purely factual learning
and training in specialized vocations are de-emphasized during
this developmental period in favour of learning structures and
principles underlying intellectual, scientific and aesthetic
disciplines.

Criteria and Illustrative Specifications

1. Participation in the planning, execution, and
   evaluation of learning

   Learners are involved in planning both school
   and out-of-school activities.

2. Individualization of learning

   Organizational facilities are provided for making
   individualized teaching and learning practicable.

3. Development of self-learning skills

   Opportunity is provided for use of a variety of
   learning resources, media and materials.

4. Development of inter-learning skills

   Learners share responsibility in the learning/
   teaching process.

5. Development of self-evaluation and co-operative
   evaluation of skills

   Group or individual work is evaluated co-operatively.

Criteria in this particular list reflect quite strongly
the curriculum orientation of the project in which they were
developed. Most of the criteria are also phrased in a way that
is relevant primarily to highly developed countries. Still,
the criteria are representative of the existing literature on
lifelong education, although it is apparent that the specific
implications of lifelong education for less developed countries
require much more exploration.

Inspection of the specifications for this cluster suggests
that at least three key assumptions about how people learn may
be inferred from the criteria. The research evidence that presently exists is not complete enough to confirm or invalidate
these assumptions, although they are widely enough held to be
influential in many attempts at educational reform.

a) If learning is individualized in pace, method,
   and content, learners will learn how to select
   and use approaches that suit them best as individuals. This knowledge will facilitate the
   development of self-direction in learning.

b) If learners are given experience in making their
   own decisions and dealing with the consequences
   of those decisions, they will become both motivated and competent to direct their own learning
   in the future. They should therefore be encouraged both individually and in groups to plan,
   carry out and evaluate their own learning program
   in an environment that offers a variety of alternative modes of learning and that is also flexible
   as to the content of learning.

c) If co-operative group learning strategies are encouraged, learners will develop lasting patterns
   of mutual support as well as inter-learning skills.

Conversely, competitive relationships among
learners and between learners and teachers will
neither develop nor become the basis of achievement motivation among some learners.

The three assumptions appear to be embedded in the conceptualization of the learning/teaching process held by many writers on lifelong education. They suggest that evaluation in
lifelong education must assess the effectiveness of patterns of
individualization, learner participation in decision-making,
and strategies for inter-learning.

V.   DEMOCRATIZATION: Equality of educational opportunity;
     opportunity to participate in decision-making and in
     the learning/teaching process despite differences in
     status; the humane exercise of authority, and the en-
     couragement of creativity, divergent thinking, flexi-
     bility and curiosity on the part of the learners.

The term "democratization" has a variety of interpretations in today's world, but there does not seem to be another
term that better sums up the elements of this final cluster.
Although the criteria in the cluster at first appear to be rather diverse, there is a common thread implied by the cluster-
label.

Criteria and Illustrative Specifications

1. Equality of educational opportunity for all regardless of personal differences

   Opportunity is available equally regardless of
   sex, race, religion, social background, and
   physical characteristics.

2. Sharing of decision-making and other types of
   involvement in the learning/teaching process
   among participants with different status and
   roles *vis à vis* the school

   Parents, community, teachers, and learners participate in school organization and administra-
   tion.

3. Humane exercise of authority

   Non-punitive evaluation functions and methods
   are stressed.

4. Encouragement of creativity and flexibility

Free creative activity, self-expression, spontaneity, and originality are encouraged.

Criteria in this cluster again appear to define what are usually thought of as educational means rather than ends. However, the latter are not hard to infer. For example, encouragement of creativity and flexibility (V.4.) would have its counterpart at the level of the learner in the orientation to Self-Growth cluster. It appears here as well because it does clearly imply a kind of democratization in the learning process. Equality of opportunity has already been cited as properly an end in its own right, although it could also be seen as a condition which facilitates growth in learners as well as in terms of its wider social implications.

The significance of the democratization theme to evaluation has already been stressed. A number of the original twenty-one principles of Faure, et al. (1972) articulate other aspects of the concept. Democratization involves creating and maintaining equality of educational opportunity. Alternative means for obtaining education should be available to all members of a society virtually throughout the active lifespan. Traditional certification procedures, especially academic marks and formal degrees, would be de-emphasized or at least placed on an equal level with alternative modes of recording progress and attainment. Individual learners and the collective public should have a greater role in educational decision-making. Traditional status barriers dividing members of the education profession from one another as well as from their students would also be loosened in order to enhance co-operative decision-making in lieu of arbitrary authority. Finally, modes of evaluation, especially at the level of the learner, which perpetuate selectivity and elitism early in life to the detriment of opportunity later on would be abandoned. These observations suggest that additional evaluation criteria relating to democratization could be developed at the organizational and societal levels.

This concludes the overview of evaluation criteria. While the criteria and especially the specifications in the multinational list deserve further elaboration and specification, the work that has been done is sufficient to illustrate the basic principles of lifelong education. The five criterion clusters of *Horizontal Integration, Vertical Articulation,*

Orientation to Self-Growth, Self-Directed Learning, and Democratization are inclusive. They incorporate what has been written on the subject and at the same time differentiate reasonably well between the most important principles of lifelong education.

Factors Affecting Choice of Perspective

It was stressed earlier that the principles of lifelong education can be interpreted from more than one perspective. The choice of perspective is likely to exert considerable influence on how one conceives of both the method and purpose of evaluation. This contains the first extensive treatment of the topic of evaluation for lifelong education and it is appropriate at least to sketch in the various perspectives that might be taken before indicating the choices that have been made here. It should be clear that such choices do have to be made if there is to be coherence and focus to the discussion.

There are two kinds of considerations that relate to how the basic function or purpose of lifelong education is operationalized in a given society. These have to do with whether (1) the society itself can be classified as highly *developed* or *developing*, and whether (2) the society is oriented primarily towards meeting the needs perceived by *individuals* as compared to the *collectivity* of individuals. A third distinction is to some degree correlated with the first, having to do with (3) whether or not the primary interest is in *formal education* as exemplified in the school or in *non-formal* or even *informal* educational delivery systems, as implied, respectively, by training on the job or the use of public television for educational purposes. Finally, two other relevant considerations relate mainly to the stance taken on evaluation itself. These are concerned with whether (4) the purpose of the evaluation is to make judgments about *learners* or about the *conditions* that affect learning, and finally, whether (5) the conception of the practice of evaluation leans toward the *research and development model* or the *human relations and/or problem-solving model(s)*. The five distinctions are interrelated, but will be addressed separately here.

Developed or Developing National Contexts

Lifelong education is likely to take on different priorities and functions in well developed as compared to less developed societies.

In less developed societies those principles of lifelong
education which offer an alternative means for achieving an educational base for the economic development of the society as a
whole may understandably have greatest appeal. Evaluation criteria that refer to what people have learned are only inter-
mediate. The real criteria have to do with social and economic
changes in the larger society. It might be much more desirable
at a given place and time to help farmers double their crops
than to teach them to read. In contrast, while social and economic criteria are not irrelevant in developed societies, much
more stress may be placed on growth of individuals in ways that
are not immediately economic in their implications. Thus the
kinds of goals education must accomplish could be qualitatively
different in developed and developing societies, and evaluation
criteria derived from these goals would differ correspondingly.

Non-formal approaches to lifelong education ordinarily
utilize rather different institutional and personal resources
in societies at opposite ends of the continuum of development.
The highly developed society is equipped with an infrastructure
of skilled individuals associated with institutions such as
schools, industry, government, and media. The institutions in
which they are employed can also provide the means of organizing
and delivering education. In the less developed countries the
institutions that must be relied on in many areas may be the
village community and the family. Individuals in such communities who act as the natural transmitters of the indigenous culture may constitute the only available infrastructure.

Evaluation tends to be shaped by the phenomena it addresses.
Methods drawn from anthropology and ethnology might be much more
useful as models for evaluation in rural areas than the research
and developmental model referred to at the beginning of this
chapter. It is also important in the case of the latter, not to
propose evaluation strategies requiring levels of technical resources and sophistication that are not likely to be available
in most developing countries.

The Individual and the Collectivity

This second distinction is related to the developed versus
developing distinction in that many, if not the great majority,
of developing countries would emphasize societal level criteria
for lifelong education. But it is also apparent that many highly developed societies can be differentiated from one another
in terms of the relative stress placed on the role of education

in the development of the individual versus the collectivity. This distinction can be made operationally in terms of the extent to which a society utilizes what may be termed a "demand" as compared to a "need" basis for allocating education resources. That is, a society may allocate educational resources more or less according to popular *demand* as contrasted with allocation of such resources in terms of the society-wide *needs* perceived by planners or other authorities. The criteria utilized for evaluation in the two kinds of system are likely to differ in the degree of stress placed on development in individuals as compared to development of the collectivity. If the two approaches were carried to the extreme, admittedly unlikely in the real world, lifelong education criteria would in the first case refer solely to growth and fulfilment experienced by individuals and in the second solely to outcomes at the level of the total society.

Formal or Non-Formal and Informal Education

As indicated above, this particular distinction is related to the earlier distinction between developed and developing national contexts. In the strict sense the principles of lifelong education incorporate both formal and alternative patterns of education equally and without emphasis on one over the other. However, in the immediate future it is likely that for highly developed societies primary responsibility for the basic school curriculum will remain within the formal educational sector. In less developed countries the reverse may be true, with basic school subjects such as reading and mathematics extensively taught in the non-formal domain. Non-formal and informal education may be the only alternative to schools that do not exist and that cannot be brought into being on a national scale as long as a low level of development continues to be a reality. The implications for evaluation of this shift in educational content between formal and informal systems are not entirely clear, but it seems likely that they are significant. Non-formal education in many of its manifestations exerts less control over the way in which people learn as well as what they choose to learn. Concomitantly, both the learners and the learning process may often be less accessible to external evaluation. The development of natural, internal evaluation capabilities would presumably be especially important in non-formal education, not only in relation to school level content, but in other areas as well.

Evaluating Learners or Evaluation of the Conditions of Learning

In the next chapter the distinction between two basic referents of evaluation, learners themselves versus the various
conditions that are designed to facilitate learning, will be
elaborated. These two activities are in many respects parallel,
though the former is a central part of the teaching process and
the latter is more identified with formal social science research. The conception of evaluation presented in the next
chapter will be comprehensive enough to incorporate both of
these basic evaluation referents.

*Research and Development or Human Relations/Problem Solving
Models*

The final distinction likely to have a bearing on how one
thinks about evaluation was implied in the three models of
change referred to briefly at the beginning of the chapter. It
is possible to conceive of evaluation as a formal and relatively systematic activity that looks to scientific method (including the non-experimental methods of social science) as the most
appropriate model for practice. Or, alternatively, evaluation
can be seen as a process of facilitating change and innovation
through example, leadership, and persuasion. In this latter
sense the social-interaction and problem-solving models of
Havelock (1971) and Huberman (1973) are more or less combined
into an approach roughly similar to what has long been known
as "action research". Here the evaluator's role involves direct participation, informal observation, and the use of human
relations skills. Both of those approaches have a place and
the choice of one does not imply that the other should not also
be explored.

Choosing a Perspective

The chapter that follows will present a comprehensive view
of evaluation in education. Its purpose is to establish a framework that incorporates concepts and distinctions to be used
throughout the remainder of the discussion. In so doing, this
book will place primary emphasis on evaluation for lifelong education at the level of the school. This choice has been made
because the school is still the dominant element in world education and will probably remain so for an indeterminate period of
time. This by no means excludes non-formal education, particularly when it incorporates some sort of institutionalized elements. It does, however, result in something of a bias toward

developed countries where the school is the dominant institutional mode.

The work on evaluation criteria presented here obviously was strongly influenced by the emphasis on criteria relating to personal development that characterizes much of the literature on lifelong education. Still, organizational and societal factors, particularly those of a structural nature, are included as well. This emphasis on criteria relating to personal development seems logical as an extension of what has been written already. It does not mean that social and economic criteria can be ignored. These remain areas that richly deserve exploration. This report also places somewhat greater emphasis on the evaluation of learners than on the conditions that affect learning simply because the former is so directly a part of the learning/teaching process.

Finally, the book depends more on the research and development model for evaluation than on the human relations/problem-solving model. However, the evaluation functions described here could be incorporated into either of the two approaches. Certainly alternative approaches to evaluation method need to be explored, although methodology is not the central topic here but rather the modes, functions, and foci of evaluation for lifelong education.

CHAPTER 2

CONCEPTUALIZING EVALUATION FOR LIFELONG EDUCATION

The purpose of this chapter is to develop a conceptualization that will assist in drawing implications about the practice of evaluation under an educational system incorporating the principles of lifelong education. In order to do this it will be necessary both to specify what are the common features of activities that are referred to as "evaluation" as well as to isolate a set of characteristics that lead to useful distinctions between various types of evaluation that differ in significant ways. The strategy here involves making distinctions from which implications about practice can be drawn. Although it has already been pointed out that all aspects of evaluation cannot be treated in detail in this report, the distinctions to be made will at least lead to a comprehensive typology or framework for all of evaluation.

Defining Evaluation

Educational evaluation incorporates a great many diverse activities and functions. Assigning marks to learners, selecting individuals for special opportunities or training, appraising the performance of teachers or the quality of instructional materials, assessing the effectiveness of various approaches to instruction, and many other kinds of activities are all commonly referred to as "evaluation". As a result, attempts to formulate neat definitions of the field with clear-cut inclusion and exclusion criteria tend to produce unsatisfactory results. It is wiser to follow the advice of Payne (1974) and propose qualitative characteristics or dimensions, all of which must be present to a substantial degree if an activity is to be described as evaluation. The four characteristics given below have been formulated so as to apply to all of the specific types of evaluation to be distinguished later (1).

Evaluation in education always involves an appraisal of the desirability of events or conditions associated with learning and teaching. The special nature of evaluation is closely tied to the appraisal of desirability. But in order to make such appraisals, information and evidence must be interpreted in terms of some value system. It has been common in much evaluation practice to ignore this underlying value base as if the grounds for establishing desirability were self-evident and universal. An evaluation theory and technology developed to serve traditional schools in a relatively homogeneous social context can of course pretend for a time that there is nothing controversial about whatever criteria are being applied. Still, even from within evaluation serious questions about this very issue have been raised of late, Stake (1973) providing a salient example.

All comprehensive views of what education should be like are built around values. Specific evaluation criteria are in turn derived from those values. Since prevailing philosophies of educational practice differ in many respects, it follows that associated evaluation criteria will differ as well. It is readily conceivable that an educational practice might be judged as desirable under one set of criteria and undesirable under another. Tractable, diligent, but teacher-dependent children might be a credit to a school in the eyes of some, while others, favouring independence and liveliness in children, would find such an outcome highly undesirable.

Evaluation is thus inevitably based on value considerations which are not empirically given and not necessarily universal. The need to interpret events in terms of desirability in part distinguishes evaluation from basic inquiry in the social sciences. The latter can often operate under the more detached perspective of description, prediction, and, where possible, explanation.

Evaluation in lifelong education cannot avoid the explicit examination of its own value base. The broad principles of lifelong education are likely to be interpreted differently in different societies, or even by groups within the same society. This is especially the case at the level of concrete evaluation criteria. The choice of evaluative criteria is in a real sense the concretization of values and as such the most critical aspect of any evaluation.

Evaluation is an experientially grounded activity carried out in a systematic and orderly manner. It was suggested at the beginning of this book that evaluation of any kind, whether casual or formal, always involves a process of "finding out". Some kind of evidence or experience is necessary as a starting point if an evaluative conclusion is to be reached. Concern here will be primarily with evaluation in its more formal aspects. That is, the types of evaluation considered will all depend on systematic examination and investigation rather than on haphazard observation or casual impression. Systematic evaluation more often than not involves the collection and interpretation of a formal, numerical type of data. However, other types of evaluative activity such as the content analysis of a written curriculum may be just as systematic and equally pertinent.

Evaluation is typically a field activity in that the information it utilizes is collected mainly in situations where learning activities occur in their natural settings. Most of the information collected in all types of evaluation evolves from what are often described as "field" or "naturalistic" settings. In contrast, basic educational research often makes extensive use of information collected in deliberately artificial, controlled situations such as the laboratory experiment. When learner performance is the phenomenon being evaluated, achievement is often measured in formal and somewhat artificial situations such as that typified by the standardized achievement test. However, even in the latter case the information generated will, it is hoped, reflect skills and capacities developed by learners in schools or other educational settings.

Almost any educational idea can be made to look successful under ideal conditions. Much can be learned in experimental demonstration schools, and evaluation has its place there as well, but generalization to the world of typical schools requires testing in that world. Evaluation in Scriven's (1967) terms may be "formative" in the sense of being concerned primarily with improving various aspects of educational programs or curricula, or it may be "summative" in the sense of rendering an overall judgment of quality. But both approaches become more and more useful as the context in which they operate approximates the context in which the program or curriculum is ultimately to be used.

Evaluation also tends to be most useful when those involved have direct contact with whatever is being evaluated. Teachers evaluating learners ordinarily have such contact. However, the evaluation of educational practice is often conducted by specialists rather far removed from the actual source of the data under appraisal. This situation is admittedly hard to avoid when the evaluation is large in scope, involving many institutions. Still, steps can be taken to mitigate the separation.

When evaluators do not have direct contact, significant events may go unnoticed. Much has been written about the importance of identifying "unintended consequences" associated with instruction. It is particularly easy to miss such consequences when goals are spelled out in advance in terms of relatively specific learning objectives and where the information collected in the evaluation reflects only those pre-determined objectives. Often relatively little is learned when this approach is taken. Scriven (1972) has even advanced the concept of "goal-free" evaluation. He suggests that real goals and objectives should be deduced directly from educational activities and materials rather than from formal statements about goals and objectives which, while designed for public consumption, may have little correspondence with reality. In this model the evaluator would remain naive as to the goals of the educational activity while collecting the data. An attempt would then be made to "guess" those goals based on what was observed. The "real" goals and the "guessed" goals could then be compared for congruency.

Evaluation is always undertaken in order to facilitate decision-making or policy formulation. This principle may appear to be something of a truism. It nevertheless deserves constant reiteration because it is all too easy to fall into the practice of collecting information merely for its own sake. Educational research (as distinguished from educational evaluation) is often conducted in order to contribute to general knowledge rather than to any particular decision needs. In contrast, evaluation should always be guided by concern for how the information is ultimately to be used and for what purpose it is to be used. Evaluation involves deliberate expenditure of time and resources that might otherwise have been assigned directly to the teaching and learning process. It must have a strongly utilitarian orientation. This does not mean that evaluations need be so rigidly planned and structured that the unintended outcomes referred to above cannot be detected.

A distinction is made here between decision-making and

policy formulation. These terms refer to levels on a hierarchy of application. Decisions are often specific manifestations of broader policies, and evaluation is relevant to both. In the understandable effort to be highly precise about the nature of evaluation a number of influential writers on the subject have developed conceptualizations which stress immediate, situation-specific information needs, and which tend to ignore evaluation for the purpose of guiding policy formulation. Stufflebeam (1968), Provus (1971) and to some extent Alkin (1969), all writers particularly concerned with the evaluation of curricula or programs, have seen the uniqueness of evaluation as lying in its close tie to educational decision-making of a very immediate kind. There is a corresponding tendency to develop evaluation models for situations in which identifiable "decision-makers" face specific "decision-alternatives".

This point has been carried further in the notion that evaluation should not attempt to generate information that is useful beyond a particular situation. Thus, Worthen and Sanders (1973) suggest that the function of evaluation be narrowed to the point where, "...the object of the search becomes non-generalizable information on performance characteristics of a specific program or process..." (p.23). This statement implies that an activity is truly evaluation if and only if its findings cannot be applied in any other situation. But this would mean that evaluation is irrelevant to the formulation of policy, since by definition the latter does generalize to a variety of situations. Certainly this limitation is unnecessarily restrictive.

Other writers, especially in the field of curriculum, have taken a broader perspective by refraining from any attempt to draw a firm line between evaluation and general educational research. Heath (1969) suggests that one of the three basic functions of curriculum evaluation *is* generalization, e.g., contributing to a body of knowledge about the design of curricula. Payne (1974) sees the distinction between curriculum evaluation and educational research as merely a matter of emphasis. This is the approach taken here. The more delimited conceptions of evaluation referred to above are nevertheless useful, especially where applied to innovative programmes being installed in schools or other highly structured situations.

Taken together, the four principles just discussed define a broad domain of functioning for educational evaluation. Each is open to great variation in degree of application. It is not surprising that individuals may disagree as to whether or not an activity is primarily evaluative or not. This does not detract from the usefulness of the principles. It merely reflects the fact that evaluation and general educational research occupy different positions on common continua.

Distinguishing between Different Types of Evaluation

There appear to be five critical characteristics which differentiate between different types of evaluation. Three of these appear to be especially important within the perspective of lifelong education. For present purposes these characteristics will be presented as defining discrete categories, in all but one case dichotomies. Later on it will be shown that all combinations of these characteristics are plausible, yielding the comprehensive classification system for evaluation referred to earlier.

In overview, the basic nature of any evaluation can be described in terms of the following:

1. *Referent*, or whether or not the evaluative judgment is to refer to the learners themselves or to the conditions that accompany learning.

2. *Level*, or aggregate level at which a decision is to be made or policy formulated, beginning with (a) individual learners, and extending through (b) organized groups of learners, (c) educational institutions, and (d) educational systems incorporating a variety of component organizations.

3. *Function*, or whether the strategy of the evaluation is (a) formative or (b) summative.

4. *Agent*, or whether the person or persons responsible for conducting the evaluation occupy (a) internal or participant roles or (b) external or non-participant roles with respect to the educational activities being assessed.

5. *Goal*, or whether the purpose of the evaluation is to assess educational outcomes which can be (a) fully specified in terms of desirable terminal states or (b) are open-ended in the sense of never being completely specifiable in terms of terminal state, possible instances, etc.

Each of these characteristics can now be defined more fully and their implications for the practice of evaluation made
explicit.

The Evaluation Referent

Evaluation incorporates two very large classes of activity
ordinarily kept separate in theory and practice. The first of
these has as its purpose the evaluation of learners themselves,
and will be referred to in the discussion that follows as *L-
Evaluation*. In this form of evaluation some sort of appraisal
is to be made about the desirability of one or more characteristics of the learner, ordinarily for the purpose of facilitating decisions that have to be made about that learner's future
activity. Sometimes this is a decision that learners make themselves, and at other times it is made by others, as will be evident when the additional distinction is made between the agents
of the evaluation. There are obviously a variety of types of
L-Evaluation including traditional academic evaluations for the
purpose of helping learners who are experiencing difficulties,
placement evaluations for the purpose of deciding at what point,
in a sequence of content, instruction should begin, and personal
evaluations that precede individual counseling.

The second basic class of evaluation referents is made up
of the conditions under which learning takes place. *C-Evaluation* assesses the effectiveness or desirability of all conditions, planned or accidental, that are potentially significant
aspects of intentional learning activity. These include the
learning/teaching process, the instructional materials, the
institutional (or non-institutional) context in which the activity is located, and the inter-action of learner characteristics with other conditions. This evaluative referent is often referred to as either "program" or "curriculum" evaluation,
though writers using the respective terms typically emphasize
somewhat different evaluative criteria. The evaluation of
teachers is implicitly included under C-Evaluation, although
it could be assigned an independent status as a third category
if it were useful to the discussion.

In many ways L- and C-Evaluation are parallel activities,
although L-Evaluation is most often conducted by participants
involved in the learning process, especially teachers and learners themselves. Systematic C-Evaluation is usually the domain
of people who are external to the learning process, frequently
with more of a researcher's, as contrasted to a practitioner's,

orientation. Still, the two types of evaluation often utilize
the same kinds of information at a different level of aggrega-
tion. But they contribute to different types of decisions, and
it is to the relationship between evaluation and decision-making
that we should turn next.

Level of Decision-Making and Policy Formulation

Goodlad (1966) has suggested that all educational decisions
can be classified within one of three different levels, each corresponding to one of the basic types of educational resources
that a society may make available to its citizens. In a more
recent treatment of this classification, Goodlad (1975) describes
the levels as "*instructional* (tutors, teachers, books, responsive
machines, for example), *institutional* (institutions whose primary
function is designated as education), and *societal* (aspects of
living having potential for serving an educational function)",
p.13.

Perhaps the most important implication of Goodlad's analysis is its recognition that direct means of delivering education
are by no means confined to interactions among teachers and
learners in the classroom. An institution such as a school can
have an impact that is more than the sum of what is occurring
in its separate classrooms. Institutions as a whole have "cli-
mates" that presumably can affect learning. Teaching and learning can even be organized on an institution wide, rather than a
classroom basis. Likewise, large systems that transcend or incorporate individual institutions such as schools, or that are
quite separate from formal schooling, may have societal outcomes that are traceable to the system as a whole.

This idea of resources and decisions at different levels
has been elaborated by Suchodolski (1970) in his concept of a
"third pedagogy". On the one hand this third pedagogy is identified with the "...contents and structure of the whole school
system in which the different schools function", a system which,
for example, may "allow an easy flow of youth to the highest
levels or which may set obstacles in the way" (2). Likewise,
"...the education of youth is not the exclusive business of
schools but is the result of activities on the part of many
other formal and non-formal entities". Both Goodlad and
Suchodolski thus suggest that direct educational impacts can
be engineered at the societal level through school systems as
well as through other systems that are independent of schooling. This same emphasis is implied in a variety of ways in

writings on lifelong education. Any comprehensive treatment of evaluation must take into account the level at which decisions and policies are to apply.

In a paper concentrating on the topic of evaluation it seems useful to make two modifications in the conceptions provided by Goodlad and Suchodolski. First, an additional distinction can be made at the instructional level where evaluation can be concerned either with the individual learner or with learners assembled in interactive groups. For example, a teacher could select a set of instructional materials for a single learner or for a group of learners. Learners could be evaluated as individuals or as co-operative learning groups where all individuals receive a mark for the group, and so on. This additional distinction has been made at the instructional level because the lifelong education literature emphasises both individual, independent learning as well as co-operative or inter-learning.

In addition it appears to be better for present purposes to use the term "system level" instead of the term "societal level" or "third curriculum". This is solely by way of being more specific about the referent of the evaluation. At this third level evaluation addresses the information needs of large systems incorporating more than one educational institution in addition to systems which, while perhaps originating in a single institutional base (television network, publisher, government agency, etc.), are widely diffused throughout a society. Evaluative conclusions are then more readily seen as pertinent to a specific system operating within a society rather than as referring to a society-wide "third" curriculum. The systems referred to here, by the way, may or may not extend through the entire society. Thus, local school systems under a decentralized educational authority would be found at the system level.

The distinction between L- and C-Evaluation and the four levels of decision-making taken together define a preliminary classification system incorporating the basic classes of decisions facilitated by evaluation. Table 1 provides examples for each of the resulting categories to help clarify what has been presented up to now.

The examples listed in the two columns of the table corresponding to L- and C-Evaluation should clarify the fact that the former always involves a conclusion about learners and the latter a conclusion about the conditions that mediate learning.

TABLE 1

A PRELIMINARY CLASSIFICATION SYSTEM COMBINING
EVALUATION REFERENT AND LEVEL OF DECISION OR POLICY ADDRESSED

Level of Decision or Policy	Referent	
	L-Evaluation	C-Evaluation
Individual	Independent learner conducts self-evaluation of own progress in achieving a goal Assessing present reading level in determining where to start a learner in e.g. a sequenced reading program	Search by an individual learner for most satisfactory way of accomplishing some learning goal Comparing effectiveness of various individualized approaches to teaching e.g. reading for learners with certain characteristics
Group	Assigning learners to learning groups so as to facilitate certain patterns of co-operation among members Monitoring actual progress of a learning group against rate of progress estimated to be appropriate	Comparing alternative patterns of grouping the members of a given class to promote learner satisfaction and progress Comparing different approaches to group study for learners with certain defined characteristics
Institution	Assessing competencies and skills of learner pool in order to establish priorities for a school curriculum Identifying and recruiting learners with defined characteristics for a local work-study program	Comparing different curriculum materials for appropriateness at schools enrolling certain types of learners Comparing different patterns of combining practical with academic learning in work-study programs
System	Identifying sub-populations needing re-training because of changes in certain work-roles National survey of independent study skills of learners at the completion of secondary school	Comparing various formal and informal modes of education in terms of utilization by a given sub-population Assessing a written national curriculum against criteria derived from the principles of lifelong eduction

There is a deliberate parallelism between juxtaposed examples in the two columns, and as a result it is probably most useful to read the two examples in each horizontal pair successively before going on to the next pair. Thus, the first pair of example has, under L-Evaluation, an individual learner assessing his or her own progress, presumably toward some personally defined goal. The corresponding example under C-Evaluation has an individual learner choosing between alternative methods of achieving a goal, implying that he or she is evaluating the conditions under which learning is to take place.

In the C-Evaluation example listed in the Table it should be clear that the decisions or policies at which the evaluation is directed are to be implemented at the level in question, but they do not necessarily apply only to the given individual, group, institution or even system in which the evaluation was conducted. In other words, the information resulting from the evaluation could be situation-specific or it could be generalizable across a variety of similar situations. The first example under C-Evaluation, group level, is specific to a particular classroom. It implies a kind of internal evaluation that a dedicated teacher might conduct. The second C-Evaluation example in the same level is intended to produce generalizations applicable to any classroom enrolling learners from the population studied in the evaluation. This merely reflects the earlier conclusion that evaluation can and does produce generalizable, in addition to situation-specific, information.

It might also be pointed out that portions of the national evaluations conducted as a part of the multi-national curriculum evaluation study reported by Skager and Dave (1977) and described in the previous chapter, fit under the last example in the Table (system level C-Evaluation). For countries involved in the study, all with centralized educational authorities, the written curriculum is of course an example of an influence that operates at the system level.

Table 1 presents what amounts to a slice or section of the full treatment of evaluation being developed here. However, the classification system in Table 1 does stand on its own in defining the basic categories of decisions addressed by evaluation. The remaining characteristics distinguish between types of educational goals, evaluation processes, and evaluation agents in ways that appear to be pertinent to lifelong education.

Formative and Summative Evaluation Functions

The distinction between formative and summative evaluation made originally in the paper by Scriven (1967), has been elaborated extensively by other writers. Probably the best argument for importance of formative evaluation is still the earlier paper by Cronbach (1963), to which Scriven's later paper was in large part a response. Cronbach, writing on the role of evaluation in "course improvement" (in present terms C-Evaluation at the instructional level), maintained that, "The greatest service evaluation can perform is to identify aspects of the course where revision is desirable" (p.676). The idea of generating information to be used for revising or improving educational practice is at the core of the concept of formative evaluation. Cronbach saw little utility in summative evaluations comparing one course against another, such as a new course or curriculum against prevailing practice. This nevertheless remains a typical approach to summative evaluation, implying some sort of final, over-all comparison of one alternative against another. Cronbach's position was that differences between courses or curricula observed in summative evaluation might easily be eliminated or even reversed if formative evaluation were used to improve one or other of the alternatives.

The concept of formative evaluation has broadened since Cronbach's paper was written. Bloom, Hastings and Madaus (1971) extended it to L-Evaluation at the individual level in their analysis of evaluation in the process of teaching and learning. Here formative evaluation concentrates on providing feedback to learners and teachers for the enhancement of learning.

Formative evaluation appears to be a much more positive and constructive function than does summative evaluation. It seeks to improve or facilitate educational practice. Summative evaluation is much more concerned with judging and selecting in both L- and C-Evaluation. Nevertheless, summative evaluation is a function that cannot be dispensed with. It is true that in the past the summative evaluation of learners by traditional academic marking systems and for the differential distribution of educational opportunity has had many negative aspects. The literature on lifelong education contains frequent references to the socially restrictive aspects of traditional grading and promotion systems (e.g. Parkyn, 1973). Some of the central proposals of lifelong education were formulated as alternatives to traditional practices in L-Evaluation. Still, many of the examples of types of evaluation in Table 1 are sum-

mative in nature. Elimination of the more negative aspects of
summative evaluation has to do in any case with the restructur-
ing of education itself.

It appears, then, that both evaluation functions are relevant to evaluation under lifelong education. Presumably there
would be a greater emphasis on the constructive aspects of formative evaluation than there is at present, especially in the
treatment of learners.

The next distinction, that between internal and external
agents of evaluation, is important because of the probably
greater emphasis under lifelong education on the role of internal evaluation agents. Internal evaluation by participants in
an educational process would tend to be formative in nature,
and this also argues for greater utilization of the formative
function.

External and Internal Evaluation Agents

Much of the earlier writing on formative and summative
evaluation has recognized at least implicitly that those who
conduct evaluations can have one of two kinds of relationship
with whatever is being evaluated. On the one hand the evaluator can at the same time participate in the educational process as a self-directed learner, as a teacher attempting to
apply or use some method or procedure, or as a developer seeking to improve learning materials or the context in which learning occurs. Part of the notion of participation is contained
in the idea that the individual in question has a role in the
situation that includes responsibilities in addition to evaluation. Participation also implies some sort of communality of
concerns and activities between evaluators and other participants. It may even imply that all participants in an educational enterprise share some of the responsibility for evaluation. One example of this will be presented in a discussion of
the advocacy model in the final Chapter. Rather than assessing
the efforts of others, *internal evaluation agents* assess the
desirability of events or conditions for which they are themselves at least partly responsible.

On the other hand, evaluators are *external evaluation
agents* whenever their responsibilities in a given situation
incorporate only evaluation. Even the teacher can be an external agent when evaluating learners in L-Evaluation, particularly when the learner is the passive object of the evaluation.

In C-Evaluation, typical evaluation practice has usually taken it for granted that an evaluator is properly an external-agent with a different and in some respects higher status than the participants in the activity under evaluation. Administrators evaluate teachers. Outside experts, from government or universities, evaluate curricula, programs, and other conditions supposed to facilitate learning. External evaluation agents are often preferred because their lack of personal responsibility for the events or conditions under evaluation presumably enhances their independence and objectivity.

It is understandable that formative evaluation tends to be associated with internal agents and summative evaluation with external agents. Formative evaluation for the purpose of improving an educational activity requires close contact with a situation and participation is one way of achieving such contact. Summative evaluation is more judgmental and often terminal. Here the objectivity of the external agent has appeal. However, there is no one-to-one relationship between the nature of the evaluation agent and the evaluation function. Evaluation agents who are external and who are responsible only for evaluative functions can and do conduct formative evaluations. Internal agents who have responsibilities in an educational process also may be responsible for summative evaluation.

It is clear that lifelong education would place much greater stress on the utilization of internal evaluation agents than has been the case in the past. The principle of *self-learning* directly implies both willingness and competency on the part of learners in regulating their own activities through self-evaluation. This is recognized by Dave (1973) who also stresses the enhanced role of the formative evaluation function, especially in L-Evaluation:

"The chief purpose of evaluation should be to improve achievement rather than just measure it for the purposes of classifying students or issuing certificates to them. Evaluation of educational achievement should be improvement oriented". (p.41)

The principle of *democratization* likewise suggests greater emphasis on internal evaluation agents under lifelong education. This principle emphasizes participation and the reduction or elimination of many types of status barriers among participants in the educational process. The concept of the internal evaluation agent is thus not restricted to self-evaluation by learn-

ers or groups of learners working co-operatively. All participants can act as internal agents, and this includes instances
of C-Evaluation in which participants in an educational process
evaluate their own attempts to create and maintain optimal conditions for learning.

There is no intent to suggest here that internal evaluation
is necessarily more valid than external evaluation, or that the
latter does not have an important role in lifelong education.
Both types of evaluation could be invalid by being based on in-
accurate information. Both could also be referenced to poorly
thought out or irrelevant standards.

Internal evaluation on the part of the learner does not ex-
clude comparison of one's work with that of others. What others
are able to do is a valuable source of information about one's
own progress, assuming that the information is not used in a
self-destructive way. But the learner in this case is still the
evaluation agent. Also, internalization of the evaluative information (as evidenced in its application or use by the learner) can occur whether the agent is internal or external. Many
would doubtless argue that internalization is much more likely
if the learner or participants are active as evaluation agents.
But seeking out the evaluations of others, getting them to serve
as external evaluators, does apply an initiating and, hence,
partly autonomous role.

Specified and Open Educational Goals

The discussion of evaluation criteria in the previous chapter made it clear that lifelong education incorporates structural and organizational goals as well as a variety of goals
relating to the personal development of learners. It was suggested that under the lifelong education framework the former
are not merely valued as "means" toward certain types of outcomes in learners, but are in fact assigned independent criterion status. Just as it is desirable to foster certain types
of personal growth in human beings, it is also desirable to facilitate certain types of development in institutions and structures associated with education. This relates very closely to
the notion just discussed of possible independent (e.g., over
and beyond events in the classroom) impacts of institutions and
larger systems on learning and learners.

OPEN-ENDED GOALS: The illustrative criteria and specifications presented in the first chapter are virtually all "open-

ended". That is, they indicate desirable directions of continuous development rather than closed, terminal states about
which it can be said with finality that a given goal has been
fully achieved. Even something so straightforward, for example,
as integration between the educational functions of home and
school is not really definable in a meaningful sense in terms
of an ideal state of home-school integration. Hundreds of *instances* of home-school integration could doubtless be proposed.
But even such a long list would probably not be exhaustive of
all the possibilities and might well include instances that
would be unacceptable in some societies and desirable in other
societies. In other words, a state or condition of home-school
integration is an ideal that can be approached but never fully
achieved, just as the limit of a mathematical function can be
approached but never reached by the curve representing that
function. It is possible to propose and recognize instances
(and non-instances) of home-school integration. It is even
possible to demonstrate that one institution or system shows
more instances of such integration than does another. But it
is not possible to state with confidence in any concrete way
what a complete or ideal state of integration between the home
and the school would be like. Anyone who was foolish enough to
attempt to do so, would doubtless threaten cultural, political,
or economic values held by large segments of the earth's population.

Integration between the home and the school is a structural
principle subsumed under the *Horizontal Integration* cluster,
but similar examples could be given for criteria from the other
clusters. Select any criterion under *Democratization*, for example, and see if it is possible to define concretely an ideal
state in which all possible instances are included and all non-
instances clearly excluded. There are many ways in which any
of these principles can be implemented, but full implementation
remains an elusive abstraction.

The same is true for goals relating to learners. The various criteria of *Self-Growth* and *Self-Directed* learning mainly
suggest ideal states that provide direction to efforts rather
than inform that a goal has been reached. The importance of
open-ended educational goals was stressed by Cronbach (1971)
in his distinction between three stages of education: (a) the
establishment of basic (though static) knowledge and skills
through training, (b) the development of intelligent analysis
and problem-solving and (c) the fostering of creative and self-
expressive production. The explicit goals of lifelong education

tend to fall into the latter two categories, although the first or basic skills category is certainly implied as well, since it is essential to the development of the other two. The latter two stages were also characterized by Cronbach's as "open-ended". Analysis and problem-solving usually allow for multiple processes of solution. Creative and self-expressive acts are not even predictable. They can be recognized when they occur (though not necessarily immediately), but they cannot be encapsulated within a definition that anticipates all of the possibilities.

There appear to be at least four possible characteristics of open-ended educational goals. Each taken alone would define an open-ended goal, but they are probably more likely to appear in various combinations, with the first characteristic probably always present. Open-ended educational goals:

1. are *continuous* in the sense of not having a concretely definable or predictable terminal point of attainment;

2. may incorporate an infinite set of manifestations by being *transferable* or applicable to a wide variety of situations and contents;

3. may represent *meta-* or *second-order* abilities that interactively combine other, less complex skills and competencies; and

4. may be represented in characteristics which combine in complex ways cognitive and affective facets of the personality leading to *self-transcendent* behaviour manifested in commitments to ideals.

The four characteristics are stated in terms of the development of the personal characteristics in learners. It should be recalled that organizational and structural goals can also be open-ended, especially in the sense of (1) above.

Open-ended goals can be measured. Chapter 4 will in part deal with the construction of definitions that lead to the assessment of instances of such goals. Appropriate definitions make it possible to recognize instances of open-ended goals when they occur and hence to count or otherwise assess their degree of attainment. But such definitions cannot specify a terminal state in which the goal has been entirely achieved nor do they predict all of the possible instances.

SPECIFIED GOALS: The first stage of Cronbach's (1971) continuum incorporates "closed" goals for which a desired state of accomplishment can be clearly stated. When applied to education the notion of something being "closed" is of course pejorative, and it seems more accurate to describe such goals as *specified*, simply because susceptibility to precise delineation is their most important characteristic. The process of specification involves making a relatively abstract goal statement more concrete by developing one or more precise rules as to how manifestations of the goal are to be recognized. Such rule-statements may refer to the actual performance of learners or to characteristics of an educational process or institution.

Specified goals by no means need be trivial. The kind of specified goals we are interested in form the basic building blocks from which higher order learning must evolve. They comprise much of the early curriculum and often encompass knowledge domains that are very large in terms of the number of elements contained. But at the same time it is true that school curricula can emphasize the achievements of specified goals that literally lead nowhere (e.g., memorizing material that does not contribute to further learning) or perseverate at this level by failing to challenge learners to develop higher order skills. Old-fashioned, rigid curricula emphasizing memorization and rote learning were of this kind. The danger is not in specified goals themselves, but rather that the curriculum might be aimed solely at this level.

The next chapter will compare several models for defining specified educational goals and also describe the various functions of L-Evaluation in the achievement of such goals. However, at least two examples of specified goals can be given here in the form of the familiar behavioral objective.

After reading an editorial taken from a nationally distributed newspaper in his or her first language, the learner will be able to select those points of view presented in the editorial from a longer list of points of view about the same topic.

This first example involves a relatively low level reading comprehension skill. It asks only for recognition rather than for production (e.g., where learners themselves generate the list without the stimulus of a prepared list). The task as defined does not require inference (assuming the editorial was clearly written) or analysis, let alone synthesis and evalua-

tion. Still, being able to recognize the basic points that a
writer is making in connected discourse is an essential step in
the development of the ability to read with understanding. The
performance is specified, but non-trivial.

Specified goals may also refer to performance at higher
levels of cognitive or affective functioning.

After reading a discussion in which the author makes
a prediction about some future event or state, the
learner will identify (by listing) the bases for the
conclusion, distinguishing between factual evidence,
argument and assumption.

The second objective requires the analysis of written material as well as the ability to distinguish between evidence,
argument and assumption. It appears to incorporate at least
two types of higher level functioning as well as the ability to
produce, rather than merely recognize, a correct response. The
objective could be elaborated with specifications as to difficulty of the reading passage, subject matter, and so on, but it
does serve to illustrate that specifiable goals can refer to
relatively high level performance.

A potential source of confusion between educational objectives derived from open-ended goals and those reflecting
specified goals lies in the fact that it is usually possible
to derive a specified objective from an open-ended goal.
For example, the *Unusual Uses Test* which is purported to measure certain aspects of creativity requires that respondents
list as many different uses for various common objects (e.g.,
a brick) as they can think of. The test is commonly scored for
the number of meaningful responses over and beyond the common
use of bricks for construction. This domain of responses is
genuinely open-ended in that unique, unpredicted responses may
always be given by individuals. There are no limits defining
the maximum possible score. However, a specified objective can
be derived for this open-ended task simply by specifying an
arbitrary standard of performance, such as the following: "The
learner will give at least five acceptable responses to the
Unusual Uses Test administered under standard conditions". The
imposition of an arbitrary limit when the test is scored for
total number of correct responses establishes a specified domain of performance with absolute limits within a much larger
open-ended domain.

The distinction between open- and specifiable goals is especially important for evaluation under lifelong education. It will be shown in the two chapters that follow that the two types of goals lend themselves to quite different strategies of evaluation, especially as related to the crediting or certifying of learner achievement.

A Classification System for Evaluation

Considered together, the five characteristics discussed in the previous section comprise a system for classifying different types of evaluation. This system appears to be applicable to evaluation operating under virtually any form of education. It is useful here as a means of identifying particular types of evaluation that would be especially important or common under lifelong education.

Referent	Level	Function	Agent	Goal
L-Learner	1-Indi- vidual	1-Forma- tive	1-Inter- nal	1-Open
C-Condi- tions	2-Group	2-Summa- tive	2-Exter- nal	2-Speci- fied
	3-Insti- tution			
	4-System			

An Evaluation Index for Differentiating Between
Types of Evaluation Based on Five Characteristics

FIGURE 1

The five boxes in the figure can be thought of as registers which might display an index combining any of the subcategories of each of the five characteristics. In all there are 64 possible combinations, far too many to illustrate here. All, however, appear to be plausible, and a few illustrations are certainly in order.

L-1111: This combination refers to a very common (and highly relevant) kind of evaluation. It has already been referred to as self-evaluation, in this case as relating to the learner's own development along some open-ended goal continuum. An individual using self-selected criteria to assess the quality of his or her own developing capacities in design, esthetic production, etc. would be engaging in this type of evaluation.

L-1121: This category of evaluation is perhaps equally common. It is illustrated whenever a teacher evaluates an individual learner's performance in some open goal area for the purpose of helping the learner improve.

L-1122: This particular type of evaluation would occur in classrooms in which teachers systematically collected information on the progress of individual learners toward the mastery of the kind of specified goals that comprise much of basic school mathematics, vocabulary, and reading skills. If it is a group that is being so monitored the closely related category, *L-2122* is seen. These important categories incorporate the kind of formative evaluation for the purpose of managing the instructional process that is the central element of several contemporary approaches to the organization of teaching and learning. Both categories will be elaborated extensively in the chapter which follows. They are by no means relevant only to the classroom. Evaluation by supervisors during on-the-job training would often fit this pattern. So do informal evaluations made by parents who are guiding the home-learning activities of their children.

L-3111: This interesting category would find an institution examining its own learners, perhaps for the purpose of assigning priorities in the curriculum. Since the evaluation agent is internal the learners would be participating in the process in some active way by helping to define goals, reporting on their own perceived strengths and weaknesses, and the like. A seemingly slight modification in this category can produce a very different evaluation situation. Thus, *L-3221* would incorporate evaluation of learners by an institution for various selection purposes. The common use of aptitude and general achievement tests for admission, grading, and the provision of special opportunities are typical examples.

L-4122: This systems level category would be illustrated by a national (or other large scale) survey conducted to identify individuals who might benefit by various kinds of educational opportunity. It is formative evaluation in that the object presumably would be to identify potential learners and guide them toward the development of personally and socially useful skills and competencies.

All of the examples so far have been confined to L-Evaluation. Parallel examples could easily be given for C-Evaluation, the difference being merely that here it is the conditions of learning rather than learners themselves that are being evaluated. For instance, the first example given (*L-1111*) when transformed into *C-1111* would be illustrated by an individual learner deciding what is the best approach to the further development of some open-ended domain of competency. This would presumably involve systematically collecting and weighing evidence as to the desirability of various alternatives. If a teacher rather than the learner were making the decision the category would change to *C-1121*. Rather than make the remaining transformations of the L-Evaluation examples already given, it would be more interesting to identify two or three of the most common varieties of C-Evaluation.

C-2112: Perhaps the majority of C-Evaluations involve comparing various educational methods, materials, etc. in terms of how they differentially affect the performance and attitudes of groups of learners. Much of the recent conceptual as well as technical writing on evaluation referred to earlier pertains to this single category and to its typical counterpart companion for summative evaluation, *C-2222*. In the first case we have an internal formative evaluation, and in the second an external summative evaluation of a program, curriculum, mode of organization and the like. This second category is probably viewed as the most relevant evaluation mode by virtually all national and international agencies funding developmental projects in education. It is also favored whenever special funding for developmental purposes occurs within educational institutions of systems. This type of evaluation is thus used particularly in the context of decisions about funding and the formulation of policy. It is dependent on external evaluation agents and is considered advantageous because of the widely perceived need for independence and objectivity in these kinds of situations.

   c-4221: This category is illustrated by any assessment of educational outcomes that is designed to reflect on the quality of a system as a whole. It could be concerned with either open or specified goals, so category *c-4222* is equally relevant here. It might involve the comparison of alternative systems, as in the case of evaluations that had been conducted in a number of countries for the purpose of comparing comprehensive versus traditional forms of education, or it might be confined to a single, total educational system. The National Assessment of Educational Progress conducted annually in the United States in recent years has focused primarily on goals of the specified variety in what Wilson (1974) describes as an attempt to provide "... *direct* measure of educational outcomes which could be utilized by school systems to improve the educational process" (p.27). These two categories of evaluation obviously have their major role at the level of policy formulation.

   At first thought it might seem unlikely that internal evaluation agents could be employed at anything so broad as the systems level and, as a result, that systems level categories incorporating internal agents would be empty. This turns out not to be the case, however. For example, a consortium of training institutions at the professional level which co-operatively assess the competencies of their own graduates in the interest of redesigning curricula would be engaging in an internal, C-Evaluation at the systems level.

   The classification system just explored does appear to highlight critical features that distinguish between the various types of evaluation. This has already helped make it easier to point out some of the considerations that would shape the practice of evaluation under lifelong education. The final section of this chapter deals directly with this question.

Implications for Evaluation under Lifelong Education

   The principles of lifelong education would have a significant impact on the practice of evaluation in ways that correspond to each of the distinctions made in the classification system. In the first case this impact would be confined to a single category of evaluation. In the other instances several categories are involved.

Four major implications for the practice of evaluation are apparent.

1. *There will be a greatly enhanced need for methods of crediting and certifying educational attainment that are not bound to particular institutions and that reflect what it is that an individual can do rather than how that individual compares to others in learning rate or other measures of academic potential.* This particular implication will be the main subject of the chapter which follows. It should be clear at the outset just what the terms "crediting" and "certifying" mean. These terms *do not* refer here to academic degrees granted by institutions as evidence that an individual has successfully met the requirements of a degree program. The latter are general documents that derive their meaning from accreditation or other formal recognition of the right of an institution to grant degrees of the traditional variety.

Rather, the two terms as used here refer to something that an individual knows or can do. The terms are differentiated in that the former refers to skills and competencies ordinarily developed in school that are at the same time useful in a variety of life roles as well as in further learning. The behavioral objectives cited earlier are examples of what is meant by academic skills and competencies for which individuals can be credited irrespective of whether or not they possess an academic degree or have ever attended a school or college. In parallel fashion, certification refers to learning that relates specifically to a particular role in the world of work. It signifies that an individual can perform a set of tasks that comprise a particular job or perhaps a component that enters into several jobs.

Crediting and certifying refer to L-Evaluation. Both are summative in nature, both require external evaluation agents, and both assess the accomplishment of specified goals and objectives. Category *L-1222* of the classification system combines these particular characteristics. This index thus defines a type of evaluation that would be of very great importance under lifelong education.

The two functions of crediting and certifying have the potential for greater flexibility as to the time, place, and manner of learning than do degree or credentialing systems associated with traditional academic institutions. This fits well with the notion of the continuous nature of learning associated

with lifelong education. Greater provision for flexible crediting and certifying systems is clearly associated with implementation of the principle of vertical articulation, as is apparent
in Lebouteux's (1973) report on the deliberations of the Pont-à-
Mousson Conference:

> "If...this new form of assessment is accompanied by
> the award of "units" or "credits" that are valid be-
> yond the school stage then the gap between school ed-
> ucation and occupational life will have been truly
> bridged...The "credits" system is giving birth to a
> new idea, that of recurrent education...the idea of
> a programme of education that begins at school but
> is carried on throughout one's life". (p.12)

The important notion in the above is that credits obtained
through schooling would not simply be accumulated toward a final degree or certificate, but would be valid after the termina-
tion of schooling. Assessment for crediting and certifying
would as a result occur more frequently in the lives of individuals than is the case at present. The possibility of having
various kinds of learning recognized in a formal way would presumably act as a motivating factor for lifelong learning.

The next and following chapters will argue that genuinely
open-ended educational goals are not compatible with the concept of crediting and certifying adopted here. Rather, these
functions will be identified with the accomplishment of specified goals and objectives. It will be suggested that a great
deal of what is important in education from the point of view
of experience and personal development would not be susceptible
to the fairly rigorous approaches to assessment for crediting
and certifying that will be presented in the next chapter. However, this by no means implies that crediting and certifying
apply only to unimportant or low-level accomplishments. It has
already been argued that specified goals are far from trivial
in education and work. There are two very significant reasons -
one pertaining to the society as a whole and the other to the
individual learner - why accurate, fair, and flexible crediting
and certification systems would be essential under a fully implemented system of lifelong education.

From the point of view of the society accurate crediting
and certification offer a vital protective shield against in-
competency and charlatanism. Lifelong education, by providing
a variety of non-formal means for educational attainment, would

at the same time tend to reduce the role traditional schools and universities have played in the maintenance of educational standards. Under these circumstances only a genuinely utopian society could afford to ignore the need to develop an alternative means for verifying educational attainment.

Certification and crediting also serve a highly important function from the point of view of the learner. These evaluation processes can guarantee that learners are judged on what they can do rather than on the time, place, or manner in which their skills were learned. Effective certification directs attention to specific competencies rather than to general school credentials. LaBelle and Verhine's (1975) summary of the large number of studies on non-formal education and occupational stratification in Latin America attests to the importance of this issue. Their findings clearly reveal that non-formal education does not enable individuals to move out of low occupational strata as long as formal school credentials constitute the primary basis for advancement. The alternative appears to be a universal, competency-based system of crediting and certification.

2. *Lifelong education would place greater stress on evaluation by internal agents for both L- and C-Evaluation.* The emphasis on democratic participation, autonomy and independent learning embedded in the principles of *Self-Learning* and *Democratization* suggests that for both L- and C-Evaluation there would be a much larger role for all categories in the classification system which incorporate internal evaluation agents. For L-Evaluation the development of motivation and skill in individual and collective self-evaluation becomes a central goal of schooling, an indispensable part of the broader educability concept. The views of Schwartz (1970) are quite representative in this regard.

> "Evaluation of the results would no longer be the prerogative of the teacher but would have to be undertaken jointly with the pupil. Everything must be done to replace evaluation by self-evaluation in the sense of 'enabling the pupil to assess himself continuously and to analyse his own mistakes'". (p.64)

Evaluation, always an important element in the so-called "hidden curriculum" of schools, would join the explicit curriculum. Learners would also be encouraged to use multiple means of evaluation.

When evaluation is internal, desirability or worth is reflected ultimately in the level of satisfaction individuals
feel about the activities in which they engage. This would be
true for internal L-Evaluation where learners are evaluating
their own activities as well as for internal C-Evaluation where
participants evaluate the conditions they have created and maintained for promoting learning. Satisfaction should not be equat-
ed with mere happiness or comfort. It has to do with accomplishment, with what Fenstermacher (1975) has described as "...endur-
ing gratification yielding a sense of worth and pride in accomplishment..." (p.238), with a sense of self-fulfilment.

3. *Under lifelong education the formative functions of*
evaluation would receive significantly greater emphasis. This
point has already been made in the earlier suggestion that categories involving both internal agents and formative functions
appear to be highly consistent with many of the comments about
evaluation appearing in the literature on lifelong education.
As far as possible evaluators are to play facilitating rather
than judgmental roles. Traditional approaches to evaluation,
especially L-Evaluation, are repeatedly characterized in terms
such as those used by Parkyn (1973) as, "...based largely on
the assumption that the school should be a selection and rejection mechanism for channeling people to different levels of a
predetermined vocational and social hierarchy" (p.31).

Traditional grading and examination systems are frequently
associated with the less egalitarian aspects of formal schooling. This view is closely connected with opposition to grading
or marking systems based on comparisons between the performance
of an individual and that of some reference group. Thus, a
1971 study of the Council of Europe on permanent education concluded that, "...the value placed on a pupil's performance
should not be based solely on the average performance of a
group of students competing against each other" (p.22). It
should be noted that the emphasis on evaluating for crediting
and certifying in (1) above is a constructive alternative to
the kinds of comparative or relative grading practices that
have been so heavily criticized in the literature on lifelong
education.

4. *The usefulness of evaluation under lifelong education*
would be significantly dependent on the development of a great-
ly enhanced capability for the measurement of goals of the open-
ended variety, especially those associated with the general con-
cept of "educability" in the case of L-Evaluation and with in-

tegrative and interactive factors in the case of C-Evaluation
The overall notion of educability sums up a variety of goals of
lifelong education with respect to the development of the individual. These goals are derived mainly from the *Growth* and
Self-Learning principles and represent a genuinely open-ended
complex of personal characteristics.

The nature of educability needs considerable elaboration
at a conceptual level before the practical measurement of its
components can be undertaken. Dave (1973) has made a start in
this direction by describing five categories of relevant learner characteristics. These will serve as a starting point for
the discussion of the educability concept in the fourth chapter.

It should be evident that the measurement of many criteria
that might be associated with educability would require careful
conceptualization followed by adequate research and development.
There are real dangers inherent in the careless application of
educability criteria for L-Evaluation. Certainly when effective
strategies do not exist for fostering aspects of growth relating
to educability, learners can hardly be held accountable for failing to develop in desired directions.

Enhancement of educability is the fundamental goal of
schooling. Educability really refers to any skill or capacity
which contributes to the potential for later learning. It is
easy enough to criticize the concept on the grounds that it
would be difficult to prove that almost any item of knowledge,
even seemingly trivial factual knowledge, could not in some way
contribute to later learning. This misses the point. There
are a number of areas in which commitment to the educability
concept on the part of schools would be recognizable in the
light of the relative emphasis given to various kinds of activities on the part of learners.

It is admittedly true that much of what would be included
in an "educability curriculum" goes on already in most schools
to at least some degree. Educators in "traditional" schools
virtually anywhere in the world would acknowledge the importance
of developing such characteristics in learners. However, it
would be difficult to find examples of evaluation instruments
and systems which are directed at more than a few educability
criteria in addition to the most concrete (even unimportant)
areas of subject-matter content. Evaluation always reflects
what is held to be important in a given place and time.

For C-Evaluation a variety of open-ended goals are implied in the Horizontal and Vertical Integration principles as well as in Democratization. These principles are structural, organizational, and sometimes interpersonal. Anything that has been said in the case of educability about the need for careful conceptualization and development of modes of assessment applies here as well.

NOTES

1. The four dimensions described here have evolved from a slightly earlier set of three presented in Chapter 3 of the report by Skager and Dave (1977) on a multinational curriculum evaluation study conducted within the life-long education perspective.

2. Translations of relevant excerpts from Suchodolski were kindly provided by Mr. Péter Inkei (see acknowledgments section).

CHAPTER 3

DEFINING AND ASSESSING SPECIFIED EDUCATIONAL GOALS IN FORMATIVE AND SUMMATIVE EVALUATION

All evaluation is concerned with accomplishment, whether attained in the past, occurring in the present, or projected for the future. But if evaluation is to be pertinent, the nature of whatever is to be accomplished has to be spelled out in the form of goals and objectives that refer to observable events or situations. Depending on how the function of education in society and in the lives of its members is viewed, goals and objectives need not always be pragmatically justified in terms of immediate economic or cost-effectiveness criteria. The concept of learning as an activity that is intrinsically worthwhile has nothing to do with cost-effectiveness, yet is compatible with many interpretations of lifelong education. But as a functional activity, evaluation cannot be conceived of as operating independently of educational goals. If the latter are not explicit in a given situation then it is the task of evaluation to find out what they are, often by inference from observations of an educational process. If goals are explicit, then one way of defining evaluation is to describe it as a process of assessing congruency between goals and events.

This and the following chapter deal with the two basic types of educational goals identified earlier. This focus has been selected with an eye on priorities. If the accomplishment of educational goals cannot be assessed, then it makes little difference what the referent, level, function, or agent of the evaluation may be. At the same time, failure to distinguish between the two types of goals could perpetuate what many writers on lifelong education have frequently deplored: the identification of evaluation, especially L-Evaluation, with the single function of selection. The kinds of certification and crediting systems that are needed to recognize and legitimate contin-

uous learning on the part of individuals and groups are properly oriented toward the assessment of specified goals only. It
should become clear in the next chapter that attempts to certi-
fy or credit performance on open-ended goals could lead to a
confusion of educational accomplishment with selective factors
such as aptitudes, social status, or cultural history.

The Importance of Specified Goals

The previous chapter described the specified educational
goal as "a desired state of accomplishment that can be clearly
stated". Specified goals refer to domains of knowledge and
skill for which states that are equivalent to full attainment
or mastery can be defined and recognized in the performance of
learners. Exactly how specified goals can be stated and full
attainment or mastery assessed are important concerns of this
chapter. But it is first necessary to address more fully the
contention that specified educational goals may be trivial or
in some other way less important than goals of the open-ended
variety. From an educational perspective the question of relative importance is not a relevant distinction between the two
types of goals, since both are essential.

One way of assessing the significance of specified goals
is to ask about their role in typical school curricula. Bloom
(1971a), as a leading spokesman for the mastery learning concept suggests that such goals are extensively represented in
school curricula and can be identified with four common types
of educational content.

1. *Required Content*. Content that is required of
   all learners is usually of considerable importance to the learner and to the society. Instruction should be designed so as to maximize
   each learner's chances of success.

2. *Sequential Content*. When content is sequential,
   each step in the learning process is dependent
   on the mastery of prior steps. Learners who
   fail to master prior steps will be unable to
   negotiate later ones even under optimum conditions.

3. *Closed content*. Closed content incorporates in
   Bloom's terms "...a finite set of ideas and be-

haviors to be learned about which there is considerable agreement among curriculum makers and
teachers". (p.34)

4. *Convergent Content*. Content requiring convergent
thinking is characterized by definite, correct
answers and appropriate processes to be used in
arriving at those answers.

The four categories of educational content proposed by
Bloom obviously overlap. For example, required content could
also be sequential in nature. The difference between closed
and convergent content is not entirely clear. But taken together the four categories reflect various ways of looking at
educational content, all of which suggest goals of the specified type.

What proportion of the content of typical school curricula
might fall into the categories proposed by Bloom? Unfortunately,
research based on content analyses of school curricula does not
appear to be available as an answer to this question. Bloom
argues that mathematical skills, language arts (presumably including reading and reading-related skills), much of science,
most second language instruction, and to some degree "mother
tongue" learning are all susceptible to mastery interpretation.
This would surely include a substantial proportion of most
school curricula.

Alternatively, what proportion of the content of typical
school curricula is either required, sequential, or both? Here
again the most reasonable answer appears to be at least a great
deal and probably most, especially at the earlier levels of
schooling. Gagné (1965) has seen all school learning as involving the development of hierarchical learning structures in
which the attainment of every capability is dependent on the
utilization of a specific set of previously acquired capabilities. This structural conception of learning leads to an analytical approach to the construction of curricula in which discrete learning steps leading to more complex objectives are
identified and carefully sequenced. Whether or not the views
of Gagné and others who follow his approach to curriculum development are accepted there can be little doubt that a large proportion of the typical school curriculum is susceptible to such
analysis.

Whenever attainment of curriculum content is required of

the general population, there is the implication that "attainment" refers to a state very similar to mastery, and that such
attainment can be assessed objectively. In other words, to require that content be "attained" assumes that educational goals
can be spelled out in some sort of concrete fashion, and that
it is possible to make reasonably accurate distinctions between
states of attainment and non-attainment. Once again, this does
not appear to be an improbable situation with regard to many
facets of the typical school curriculum. If attention moves
from skills usually developed in schools to skills required in
a given field of employment, a similar situation prevails. Concrete, specified learning goals can be stated for most skilled
and unskilled industrial jobs as inspection of modern industrial
and technical training manuals would readily show. The latter
often sequence content in a hierarchial fashion. Even highly
skilled professional work roles usually incorporate an array of
specific competencies and capabilities that can be specified
quite concretely. If this seems doubtful, consider what professional roles as different as medical doctor and airline pi-
lot actually require of their members. Competencies in a great
many specific "tasks" that such skilled professionals are required to perform in the course of their work can be assessed
objectively. This is not to say that everything that medical
doctors or commercial pilots do merely reflects the attainment
of a set of virtually automatized learning structures. But it
does suggest that the foundation of much highly complex performance in work consists of an organized set of specific skills
and competencies for which full attainment or mastery can for
practical purposes be clearly established.

In spite of arguments to the contrary by Ebel (1971), it
does appear that both academic and vocational curricula are
likely to include a significant proportion of specified educational goals. Here what is being dealt with are admittedly
the most definable and tangible outcomes of education, but such
outcomes are hardly less vital simply because they are susceptible to clear specification and mastery interpretation.

Evaluative Functions at the Level of the Learner

Another way to assess the importance of specified educational goals is to view them in relation to the basic functions
of evaluation in the learning/teaching process. These functions are listed in Table 2.

TABLE 2

L-EVALUATION FUNCTIONS IN THE ORGANIZED LEARNING SITUATION

Formative		Organizing and carrying out the learning and teaching process in a manner that is maximally adaptive to the characteristics of the learners.
	Diagnosing	Determining the most appropriate approaches to learning (learning strategies and conditions, instructional materials, etc.)
	Placement	Determining the point(s) in the curriculum at which learners should begin.
	Monitoring	Keeping track of the progress of learners to determine whether the approach to instruction should be changed whether learners are ready to move on to new content, etc.
Summative		Assessing and recording what the learners have accomplished
	Crediting	Establishing and recording that learners have achieved a state of full attainment in some defined curriculum content domain.
	Certifying	Establishing and recording that learners are able to perform some socially useful activity according to formally defined and officially recognized standards.
	Selecting	Making comparisons among learners on the relative quality of their performance for the purpose of assigning marks, providing special opportunities, etc.

The L-Evaluation functions in this table are divided into the two major categories of *formative* and *summative*, with the former referring to decisions that affect the learning process itself, whether made externally by teachers or internally by learners themselves, and the latter to the compilation of records about what learners have achieved or what they can be predicted to achieve. These are of course more specific instances of the general distinctions between formative and summative evaluation made in Chapter 2.

Formative evaluation functions are divided into *diagnosis*, or finding the approach to learning that is most appropriate for an individual learner or group of learners with similar characteristics (see Glaser & Nitko, 1971), *placement*, or deciding at what point in the curriculum to begin, and *monitoring*, or determining whether or not learning is proceeding at a satisfactory rate and in a fashion that is appropriate for the learner. The latter evaluation function contributes to decisions about changes in the learning mode as well as the pacing of the learning process as learners move through the curriculum.

The summative evaluation functions incorporate *crediting* for school-level learning and *certifying* for ability to perform some integrated work activity, plus the third function of *selecting*. The latter usually involves making a judgment about the learner that is based on comparisons with other learners. Academic grades are normally generated from comparisons between learners, as are objective indices such as IQ scores and percentile or other normative scores on objective tests of educational achievement. This kind of information is frequently used to predict future performance in situations in which only those who are expected to do well are to be selected. Often the actual selection occurs only long after the original comparison was made, as when admission to higher education is based on prior academic record.

When, then, do specified goals fit into this functional analysis of evaluation in the learning process? As anticipated above, the relative importance of assessing for full attainment or mastery is directly related to the theory of education under which evaluation is operating. Under a highly selective and elitist approach to education, L-Evaluation tends to emphasize assessment for the purpose of making comparisons among learners as to their standing relative to one another. Here the assessment of full attainment or mastery is unnecessary since the only function for L-Evaluation is to determine which learners

perform best. Under such an approach (in its extreme form) the
single summative function of selecting is significantly more
emphasized than the other evaluative functions in Table 2. Diagnosis for the purpose of determining the most effective mode
of learning and placement of learners at an appropriate point
in the curriculum sequence are irrelevant in situations deliberately structured so that every learner must negotiate the
same obstacle course. Likewise, the summative functions of
crediting and certifying are of little importance. The issue
is not what a learner knows or can do, but rather how that
learner stands in relation to others.

Under a different philosophy about the nature and purpose
of education the functions of evaluation at the L-level change
dramatically. The lifelong educational principle of democratization stresses that opportunity for learning is to be extended throughout a society and without regard to differences
between individuals in rate of learning and preference for
where and how learning takes place. This principle argues
against the identification of evaluation with selection and in
favor of an evaluation practice whose purpose is to facilitate
the learning process as well as to recognize attainment whether
or not that attainment occurs in a formal or non-formal educational context.

The strongly egalitarian conception of the role of education in society that is identified with lifelong education
would render the assessment of full attainment or mastery of
specified educational goals essential to four of the six of the
L-Evaluation functions of Table 2 and useful, though not unique-
ly so, for a fifth.

Diagnosis. This first formative function is the only type
of L-Evaluation in the learning situation for which the assessment of specified learning goals appears to be mainly irrelevant. Decisions about how a given learner or group of learners should go about attaining a given domain of educational
content are not likely to be directly facilitated by the knowledge that other domains of content have already been attained.
Here the problem is one of determining the mode of learning and
the context in which learning should occur. The fact that some
other domain of content was mastered by a learner under traditional group instruction does not mean that that particular
mode of learning is either the most efficient or the most compatible. The learner's personal preferences, prior experiences,
special aptitudes, interests, and social/emotional needs are

likely to be determining factors in diagnostic decisions. These characteristics are more associated with the personality of the learner than measures of educational achievement, whether of the specified or open variety.

Placement. The point at which the learner is to begin in a curriculum sequence can only be established by finding out what that learner already knows. The assessment of specified learning goals prerequisite to the content in question appears to be the most direct and accurate means of accomplishing this function. All but one of the concrete examples of facilitative learning systems to be reviewed in the next section do base decisions about placement solely on the attainment of specified goals. Some questions about possible consequences will be raised in the case of the single system which apparently derives placement decisions from measures of learner aptitudes.

Monitoring. It is difficult to conceive how the monitoring function could be carried out in a systematic and accurate manner without assessing the learner's progress on specified learning goals. The crucial information here is whether or not the learner has mastered the content in question. Decisions about moving on to a new unit of content or, if mastery has not yet been attained, instigating review or changing the mode of learning all hinge directly on this kind of information. All of the examples reviewed in the next section assess specified learning goals for this purpose.

Progress in learning is not the only consideration entering into the monitoring function. The learner's level of satisfaction with the mode and context of learning should also be an important consideration, though one that does not involve assessing attainment directly. The evidence Bloom (1971b) presents for the relationship between attainment of mastery and task satisfaction, as well as evidence relating mastery to positive self-concept as a learner, argues that an important relationship exists between performance and the learner's satisfaction with the mode of learning.

Crediting and certifying. Under the definitions adopted in the previous chapter, these two summative evaluation functions refer solely to the assessment of specified goals. In the educational examples about to be discussed both functions are confined to reports (e.g., to parents) on learner accomplishment. The full utilization of the crediting and certifying functions can of course occur only under wider educational credentialing systems that are not tied solely to traditional institution-bound academic degrees and diplomas.

Selection. The final summative function at the level of the classroom ordinarily involves making comparisons between learners in terms of *rate* or *amount* of learning. If time for learning is held constant for all learners, these two criteria add up to approximately the same thing. The number of specified goals accomplished over a given period of time as compared to the number accomplished by other learners could certainly serve as a measure of quality (or quantity) of learning, and indeed does so in the case of at least one of the examples to be discussed.

Typical contemporary practice seldom bases evaluation for selective purposes on the assessment of specified learning goals. Achievement tests, especially those designed to assess learning over fairly long periods of time, are designed to spread learners out on a continuum. In order to do so it is convenient to construct such tests in a way that makes it highly unlikely that any learner will answer all of the questions or exercises correctly. Likewise, transfer of learning to previously unencountered problem situations is often of interest when "quality" of learning is being assessed. These kinds of test construction practices lead inevitably to the assessment of educational goals of the open variety. While Skager (1971) and others have argued that achievement measures of this type are frequently used for many L- and C-Evaluation functions for which the kind of information they provide is inappropriate, they do have many other legitimate uses as Sax (1974) has pointed out.

Under lifelong education the importance of assessing the attainment of specified educational goals would appear to be greatly enhanced. Indeed, without objective systems for crediting and certifying learner achievement it is unlikely that patterns of flexible, long-term learning associated with lifelong education would ever become a common mode of adaptation within any society. Such systems would focus on the skills and competencies that individuals actually possess rather than on where or how those skills and competencies were obtained. Likewise, L-Evaluation for the purpose of facilitating the learning process would depend heavily on information about the attainment of specified learning goals.

Assessing Specified Learning Goals in Adaptive Learning Contexts

A major thrust of recent educational thought and research has been concerned with the creation of learning contexts characterized by what Glaser and Nitko (1971) refer to as "adaptive" instruction. This concept is not identified with any particular model of teaching, but rather with a variety of approaches derived from two assumptions: (a) the great majority of learners can fully attain or master the basic school curriculum, and (b) such attainment will occur if the teaching and learning process is sufficiently adaptive to the needs and learning styles of individual learners or group of learners with similar characteristics.

Although originating primarily in psychological learning theory and educational technology, various approaches to adaptive learning are remarkably congruent philosophically with a number of aspects of the democratization principle of lifelong education. This is readily apparent in the early part of Bloom's (1968) adaptation of Carroll's (1963) model of school learning to the concept of "learning for mastery". It is also evident in Glaser and Nitko's (1971) characterization of traditional or "nonadaptive" instruction as based on the assumption that "...not all pupils can learn a given instructional task to a specified degree of mastery" (p. 645). In the past individual differences in learning rate, aptitudes, prior skills, willingness to persevere, and attitude toward learning have indeed seemed to offer a self-evident basis for the selective distribution of educational opportunity. In addition, Dahllof's (1973) research suggests that traditional instruction is usually designed for a kind of "standard" learner occupying a position somewhat below the class median in overall academic ability. Instruction so directed is likely to meet the individual needs of only a few.

Adaptive Instruction in Higher Education

Bloom (1971a) and other advocates of mastery learning principles maintain that when all learners are allowed the same amount of time for learning and must use the same materials and modes of study, there will invariably be a high correlation between achievement and the characteristics learners bring to the situation. The more the learner knows in advance and the higher his or her level of aptitude for the task, the higher will be that learner's achievement relative to other learners. By optimizing quality of instruction favoring the individual learner and by maintaining flexibility as to the time allowed for

learning, this typical relationship for those who are best prepared may be disrupted.

This proposition was tested by Arasian (1972) in an application of the mastery model to a typical course at the university level. The basic elements of the model are evident in the
following steps derived from Arasian's report on the research.

1. The competencies and skills to be developed by
   students by the end of the course were spelled
   out carefully so that tests could be constructed
   that measured precisely the objectives of instruction.

2. At the beginning of the course students were given
   a diagnostic examination measuring all of the objectives of the course in order to determine their
   level of prior knowledge.

3. Every two weeks during the course students took
   diagnostic tests measuring their attainment of
   the objectives during that period. Items or questions answered incorrectly by more than half of
   the students were identified, but scores on these
   diagnostic tests for individual students were not
   seen by the instructor.

4. Students were encouraged to form small groups to
   study content areas relating to test questions
   missed by more than half of the class.

5. At the end students took a final examination covering the entire content of the course. They were
   assured that any student attaining the criterion
   score established for mastery would receive the
   highest possible mark.

Arasian reported that during the previous year of the
course, before the above procedures had been adopted, only
about 30% of the students attained the mastery criterion. In
contrast, for the class participating in the study about 80% of
the students attained the same criterion. At the beginning of
the experimental course there was a moderately high correlation
(approximately .6) between the general diagnostic examination
given at entry and performance on the first two-week unit test.
By the time the last two unit tests were administered, this

correlation had dropped to zero. Informing students about gaps in their learning and initiating special, co-operative study procedures appeared to have eliminated the relationship between prior knowledge and final performance. This finding is consistent with Block's (1970) observation that the effect of pre-existing individual differences on attainment could be drastically reduced or even eliminated under mastery learning conditions.

An Adaptive Instructional System in a Developing Country

The Korean Educational Development Institute has designed an adaptive instructional system at the elementary and middle school levels in response to deficiencies in traditional school programs in that country. Kim, Cho, Park, and Park (1974) noted three areas of needs to be addressed by the system: (1) *materials* in addition to conventional textbooks, including programmed texts and workbooks that students could use independently, evaluation materials for assessing learner progress, and manuals for teachers describing teaching and learning activities appropriate for each unit of the curriculum; (2) *alternative teaching processes* that would permit adaptations in the mode and pace of instruction to meet the needs of learners with differing characteristics (as contrasted to gearing instruction to the "average" learner), coupled with regular evaluation procedures for determining whether learners have mastered prerequisites to each unit of the curriculum; and (3) *utilization of educational technology* to supplement the activities of teachers, especially educational television as an alternative mode of instruction in the classroom.

The system developed by the Institute was based on a five-stage model of the learning/teaching process. These stages incorporate typical components of adaptive instruction.

PLANNING. The curriculum was divided into units, each with clearly stated "terminal" objectives specifying what learners who have mastered the unit should know and be able to do. Each unit so defined was subjected to a task analysis identifying the various steps or components within the unit that would have to be attained en route to mastering the terminal objective. These steps within units were then sequenced à la Gagné (1965). Finally, an instructional plan for teachers was developed describing the unit steps, their sequence, and the instructional approach or an approach that might be used.

DIAGNOSIS. Diagnostic tests appropriate to the initial
period of instruction (e.g., beginning of the school year or
major topics) were constructed for assessing learner deficiencies in the prerequisites for each subject matter area. Results
of these tests were used to determine what kinds of remedial
instruction would be required before beginning on the main topic. A portion of this instruction was given by teachers in the
classroom and the remainder assigned to independent study using
remedial materials incorporated in student workbooks. It should
be noted that this particular tactic of providing remedial instruction before beginning the main topic is really one way of
accomplishing the placement function of Table 2 (1). However,
once the remedial learning phase is completed, all learners
begin work on the main topic at the same level and point in
time.

TEACHING-LEARNING. The main phase of study on a given
topic or segment of the curriculum was standardized for all
learners in terms of modes of instruction and time spent on
task. However, instructional mode was varied within and between units and included discussion, lecture, programmed instruction, utilization of workbooks, and some instructional
television. Formal evaluation of learner progress did not occur in this stage.

EXTENDED LEARNING. This fourth phase of the KEDI system
incorporates a variation of the formative evaluation function
of monitoring. In this particular approach relatively short
formative tests were administered to all learners in order to
identify the kinds of remedial and supplementary work that
might be required. Learners were informed that the test results would be used for instructional purposes rather than for
grading. Following instruction in their guides, teachers divided learners into mastery, near-mastery, and non-mastery
groups. During the learning phase which followed, students
who had attained mastery worked independently on enrichment
materials provided in the workbooks. Near-mastery learners
also worked independently, but with supplementary materials in
the workbooks. Non-mastery learners were taught directly by
the teacher using appropriate supplementary material. Individual work by the first two groups was checked by the teacher.
The extended learning and perhaps the diagnostic phase are the
only points at which some degree of individualization of instruction is incorporated into the KEDI system. This suggests,
perhaps surprisingly, that a high degree of individualization
is not the essential element in adaptive instruction. This

observation is important. Extensive individualization of teaching and learning is ordinarily associated with a high degree of expertise on the part of the teacher as well as costly support services and materials. The Korean system was obviously developed under practical limitations imposed by the fact that it would have to be used by teachers working alone in traditionally organized classrooms.

EVALUATION. In the final phase of the KEDI system (after instruction is terminated) summative tests are administered for the purpose of assigning grades to learners. It has already been pointed out that academic grades of a comparative nature are ordinarily used for differentiating among individuals in terms of rewards, status, or opportunity. The summative evaluation function incorporated in this last phase, therefore, appears to be selection rather than crediting or certification. This is by no means inevitable in the light of the other characteristics of the KEDI system. In a national educational system organized according to lifelong educational principles, crediting and certifying would replace selection as the dominant summative evaluation function for an adaptive learning system such as that developed by the Korean Educational Development Institute.

Overall, the KEDI system is a useful example of adaptive instruction operating within the practical limits of traditional classroom structure and finite resources. While it may be true that the system utilizes special materials such as workbooks, teacher's guides, and evaluation devices, the principle cost of such materials is in the initial development phase. This particular system utilizes educational television to some extent, but this technological element is not an essential component in the operation of the system.

The diagnostic and the extended learning phases of the KEDI system definitely depend on the assessment of specified learning goals. It is not clear from Kim, Cho, Park and Park (1974) whether this is the case for the last, or evaluation phase. An academic grading system could be based on differences among learners in the number of specified goals fully attained over a given period of time as reflected on a summative test. Alternatively, summative tests used for selective grading practices may not be referenced to specified goals at all, as is the case for typical contemporary tests of educational achievement.

Individualized Adaptive Instructional Programs

The most fully elaborated forms of adaptive instruction incorporate a variety of tactics for individualizing the learning experience. While the focus here is on evaluation rather than on instruction, both activities are closely interwoven in a fully individualized learning situation. Individualized instruction depends on all of the formative evaluation functions listed in Table 2. The diagnostic function emerges as especially important since the conditions of learning cannot be adapted to the needs of individual learners unless some method is available for determining which conditions are most appropriate.

It should be admitted at the outset that extensively individualized instruction, at least in its contemporary forms, implies greater complexity with respect to the teacher's role and requires materials and support services that even in developed societies exceed what is available in the typical school classroom. In this respect the educability concept associated with lifelong education has a pragmatic basis. To the extent that autonomy and independence in the learning process are developed in learners, it would be unnecessary for teachers to spend such a large proportion of their time functioning as external evaluation agents. But for purposes of illustration, individualized approaches to adaptive instruction articulate most fully the various ways in which adaptive instruction depends on the assessment of specified learning goals.

Attempts to individualize instruction are of course hardly new. The 1920s saw early implementations of the concept identified with Washburne (1922) and Morrison (1926) that embodied most of the essential elements of today's models. Curricula were sectioned into discrete sequenced units with mastery the criterion for progression from unit to unit. While the approaches identified with these authors differed in some respects, both utilized progress tests at the end of each unit. Results of the tests revealed which elements of content had not been mastered. Learners were redirected to the gaps in accomplishment through practice on self-instructional materials, tutoring, or other approaches, depending on which of the two models was being applied. One of the models was entirely learner self-paced.

These early approaches to individualization attracted considerable interest for over a decade, but did not ultimately result in widespread implementation. Block (1971) attributes

this outcome to the unavailability of technical aids capable of
sustaining implementation at a general level. While there may
be reasons other than the one Block proposes, many contemporary
systems do make extensive use of technical aids, especially in
relationship to the various evaluation functions. This is illustrated in Hambleton's (1974) comparison of three of the most
developed systems for individualizing instruction: *Individually
Prescribed Instruction* (IPI), described by Glaser (1968); *Program for Learning in Accordance with Needs* (PLAN), in Flannagan
(1967, 1969); and *Learning for Mastery* (LFM), reported in Block
(1971). Since Hambleton has already compared the basic feature
of the three programs in some detail, the emphasis here will be
on the ways in which each program manages the L-Evaluation function of Table 2.

The three systems are offered as concrete examples. Neither
singly nor collectively do they approach a full representation of
lifelong education at the level of the learner. However, they
do place considerable stress on the important principles of individualization and flexibility. Each also makes extensive use
of various types of L-Evaluation as regulatory mechanisms in
the learning/teaching process. In fact, each system can accurately be said to have been built around the L-Evaluation functions listed in Table 2.

LFM differs from the other two systems in that it is really a set of principles and procedures derived from Carroll's
(1963) model of school learning and Bloom's (1968) translation
of that model into the concept of learning for mastery. PLAN
and IPI, while also based on learning/teaching models, are
transportable instructional packages complete with instructional materials, evaluation devices, and guides for teachers. Essential features of the three systems in the light of the six-
L-Evaluation functions of Table 2 are abstracted in Table 3.
These contrasts will be elaborated briefly.

With the single exception of the formative function of
diagnosis of learning mode, virtually all of the other evaluative functions in the three systems appear to involve the assessment of specified learning goals. As was the case for the
relatively non-individualized approaches to adaptive instruction described earlier, all three of the individualized systems
divide the curriculum into sequenced units or objectives for
which full attainment or mastery is to be the goal for all
learners, just as it was under the lifelong education principle
of democratization. Only the PLAN system adds additional ob-

TABLE 3

SUMMARY OF L-EVALUATION COMPONENTS IN THREE HIGHLY
INDIVIDUALIZED, ADAPTIVE APPROACHES TO INSTRUCTION

L-Evaluation Function	IPI	Plan	LFM
Diagnosis	Method of instruction assigned through judgments about past performance, potential, etc.	Similiar to IPI, but assigns instructional method (teacher-learner unit) with aid of computer	Group instruction used for all pupils initially, then individualized in different instructional *modes* where needed
Placement	Initial *placement test* covering all units at appropriate level used to prescribe program for individual learner, and unit pretests to select objectives within units in program	*Modules* selected for personal program of study based on pupils', parents' *long-range goals* and systematic information from "Developed Aptitude Performance Tests"	Course objectives common to all learners, combined into units
Monitoring	*Unit Posttests* for exit from unit and *curriculum-embedded tests* monitoring progress on each objective in unit	Posttests at end of each module covering several objectives, pretest optional	*Diagnostic progress tests* given at posttests covering each unit combining several objectives
Crediting/ Certifying	Report on number of units mastered recommended, no special end of course test	Similar to IPI	*Summative tests* for mastery of total set of objectives of course
Selection	Grades based on credits attained (if required locally)	Similar to IPI	Grades based on summative test performance, if possible locally on basis of accomplishment of learner rather than comparison with others

jectives ("module-set objectives") which incorporate concept development and types of problem solving that possibly represent open-ended, rather than specified, educational goals. Progress on the latter is regularly assessed, although separately from the assessment of progress on specified objectives comprising the core modules of the curriculum.

DIAGNOSIS. Selection of the most appropriate mode of learning for IPI is a relatively informal process utilizing information normally available to teachers, including information about a given learner's preferences and earlier performance. In PLAN the opposite is true. Diagnosis for the purpose of selecting the mode of learning is based on the same predictive test that is used in designing the learner's program of study.

Under LFM learners select their own approach to learning only in the case of supplementary study. Initial instruction on each unit of the curriculum is group based. At the end of the initial period of group instruction *unit posttests* (formative) are used to identify learners who have not fully attained the unit. (This is of course assessment under the monitoring function falling under the next category.) Learners so identified can select from various learning modes including small group work, tutoring, or alternative kinds of individual work materials.

Allowing learners to choose their own modes of learning is especially appealing in the context of lifelong education. It seems reasonable to hypothesize that self-direction in learning is likely to develop only in situations in which learners have the responsibility for making their own choices. Furthermore, Cronbach's (1975) recent review reveals that a sufficient research base for matching learners with learning mode does not currently exist. The PLAN program, which presumably makes use of existing knowledge, probably deserves careful scrutiny with respect to this function. Encouraging learners to select their own learning mode and to evaluate the outcomes of those choices seems potentially more beneficial and perhaps even more realistic today. Obviously, the level of experience of the learner or the interference of learning disabilities would have to be considered in the kinds of choices that are provided.

PLACEMENT. IPI incorporates two types of placement evaluations. The *placement test* covers the most representative or difficult objectives within each level of the curriculum, and its results are used to design the learner's overall program of

study. Typically, units are assigned when a learner's placement score on representative objectives falls between 20 and
80% correct. Learners scoring below this range would be assigned units at an earlier level in the content area. Those
scoring above would be assigned units at later levels.

The second IPI placement test identifies objectives within
an assigned unit that have already been mastered by the learner.
This unit pretest is not incorporated in the other two programs.
Its function is to avoid having learners spend time on material
which learners who spend time on content have already attained.
On the other hand, the use of such tests obviously adds to the
time devoted to assessment. In a fixed-time instructional system this assessment time is subtracted from learning time.

PLAN utilizes a unique approach to placement. A "Developed
Abilities Performance Test" helps parents and students select a
long-range goal from 12 basic occupational categories. This
process involves statistical matching of the learner's relevant
personal characteristics with those of members of the 12 occupational categories. Once the long-range goal has been set, a
year-long program is planned for the learner. The number and
type of learning modules to be covered are also derived from
predictions based on the performance test. The PLAN program
in this and other functions depends on the use of a computer
and other technical back up. The test itself is designed for
predictive purposes rather than for the measurement of specified learning goals. In fact, the purpose of this particular
assessment is to "place" the learner at the beginning of an *individual* curriculum rather than at a point within a curriculum
common to other learners.

The LFM model as described by Block (1971) does not conduct placement testing. Curriculum content is the same for all
learners, and instruction on each unit begins in the group mode.
Only later on is the learning mode individualized for those students who did not master the unit during the initial period of
group instruction. Of the three programs, LFM requires the
least testing and in other respects incorporates the most eco-
nomical approach to individualization.

MONITORING. IPI utilizes two types of tests for the monitoring function. The "curriculum-embedded" test is referenced
to the smallest unit of instruction - the single learning objective. Several such tests, each consisting of a very few
items, are available for each objective so that learners who

have not mastered the objective on the first or second attempt can take a new test on which they have not had a chance to practice. Passing the curriculum-embedded test allows the learner to move on to the next objective in the unit. When all of the objectives have been learned, a unit posttest covering the entire unit is administered. Decisions about changing the mode of instruction or repeating earlier material are based on these results.

In PLAN, learners elect to take a module posttest whenever they feel they have mastered all of the objectives in the module. Performance on this measure determines whether it is time to move on to the next module in the learner's program or better to select among several types of review work. Information from module posttests is supplemented by periodic administrations of achievement tests covering the curriculum as a whole. It is not clear from published sources exactly how results from the latter are utilized.

LFM also utilizes unit posttests referred to as *formative tests* or *diagnostic-progress tests*. They are used to prescribe individualized study on a supplementary basis for objectives that have not been mastered. Such tests are assumed to provide additional practice for students who have mastered the unit, reinforcing learning. All three programs thus make use of some type of unit testing for the formative function of monitoring. This appears to be an essential feature of evaluation in mastery learning.

CREDITING/CERTIFYING. All three of the programs have been implemented in schools and have, therefore, been concerned with crediting achievement of school content rather than certifying competency in purely work skills. IPI and PLAN operate in a similar fashion. In both cases comparisons characteristic of traditional academic grades are avoided insofar as possible. Reports to students and parents are based simply on the number and nature of units mastered. Referencing of learner performance to the curriculum rather than to the accomplishments of other learners is an essential characteristic of the crediting/certifying function as initially explored in the previous chapter. However, both IPI and PLAN have been developed within a national educational system that mainly depends on traditional academic marks leading to diplomas and degrees awarded by formal educational institutions. In other words, the direct, noncomparative crediting that these two programs use for reports on learner performance does not go beyond the report to parents and ultimately contributes to a traditional school certificate whose validity is established by the standing or accreditation of the institution rather than directly reflecting the learner's attainment of the curriculum. Still, both programs clearly utilize the summative function of crediting at the grade or course level. This does not appear to be consistent with equality of opportunity, an important aspect of the principle of democratization.

The approach taken by LFM to the summative evaluation is less easy to classify as either crediting or selection. A summative test covering the entire curriculum is administered at the end of the course. If the results of this test are used to establish grades reflecting relative comparisons among learners, then this is clearly an evaluation that is tied ultimately to selection. This may well occur with LFM depending on the orientation of the user. There is a suspicion that it could also be the case for the other two programs, in spite of intentions to the contrary on the part of their developers.

Summative L-Evaluation for purposes of selection runs counter to the philosophy underlying LFM. Bloom (1971a) clearly prefers that performance evaluations be based on what the individual has accomplished rather than on comparisons with other learners. This suggestion is not easy to implement in a purely crediting sense. Diligent but slow learners who accomplish relatively less than other learners would still be graded low unless some sort of correction factor were applied. Likewise, providing information on the number of units attained by a child does not bar the child, parent, or teacher from developing a comparative interpretation referenced to the number of units attained by other learners. It was noted earlier that a major goal of all highly individualized learning programs is to reduce or even eliminate individual differences in amount learned by optimizing the conditions under which learning takes place. Block's (1970) report suggests that significant reductions are possible, although it seems highly unrealistic to expect that all differences can be eliminated without somehow slowing down the very rapid learner. The latter course is not seriously proposed by anyone. Still, all three of the programs de-emphasize summative evaluation of the selected variety in favor of some form of crediting for the accomplishment of specified learning objectives.

SELECTION. It should be clear from the above discussion that any kind of report on student attainment, even if stated purely in terms of number of units accomplished, can be used to compare one learner with another and as a result contribute to some kind of selection. Whether or not such comparisons occur for any of the three programs depends on the information needs of the user rather than the intentions of the developers and conceptualizers.

PLAN at least potentially incorporates another type of summative evaluation for selective purposes, one that is far more subtle than overt practices such as assigning academic grades. The "Developed Abilities Performance Test" used to establish a "long-range goal" for the learner is clearly an instrument constructed for predictive purposes. This particular prediction is derived from an estimate of how similar the learner is to members of each of the 12 occupational groups. Now, it is unlikely that all 12 groups are of equal status socially, educationally, or occupationally. By gearing the learner's curriculum to a particular occupational group, it seems inevitable that some kind of implicit selection will occur. If the prediction derived from the test is a reasonably valid one, then this may be a good or a bad practice depending on the point of view. If the prediction has little or no long-term validity, then this practice would be bad from anyone's point of view. In any case, by designing a curriculum for a learner's predicted future occupational classification, PLAN is possibly injecting a type of selection into the process of individualizing instruction. Moreover, this potential summative evaluation occurs before, rather than after, instruction begins.

Implications

The examples of adaptive approaches to the learning/teaching process that have just been discussed vary significantly in the degree to which instruction is individualized, in the use of technological aids, and in the manner and extent to which the functions of L-Evaluation are applied. In presentation the various approaches were deliberately ordered from the simple strategy devised by Arasian (from the flexible LFM model) to the complex instructional systems embodied in IPI and PLAN. The essential role of specified educational goals in all five of the examples discussed should be abundantly clear. Instruction that is genuinely adaptive to the needs of learners depends almost entirely on the assessment of specified learning goals in order to carry out two of the three functions of formative evaluation. Concomitantly, certifying and crediting in summative evaluation must be referenced to specified goals if recognition is to be given for actual accomplishment rather than for relative standing in comparison to other learners.

This capability is vital for the implementation of lifelong education. Crediting and certifying will have to be based on accurate measurement of what individuals actually know or can do, rather than on how they stand with respect to their peers within a particular type of educational institution. Otherwise, learning by non-formal and informal means will inevitable go unrecognized by the society at large.

It should be noted that in the IPI and PLAN programs decision-making relating to the L-Evaluation functions tends to be assigned to teachers or other authorities. This emphasis does not mesh with the stress placed by lifelong education on self-direction in learning. However, the broader concept of adaptive instruction in no way argues against the assignment of significant responsibility to the learners. It simply was not a major consideration to the designers of these particular programs. Carroll (1971), by contrast, reports observing a LFM program in which even very young learners conducted their own formative evaluation and completed each unit by tutoring another student.

Up to this point the key concept of full attainment of mastery as applied to specified goals has been used without any attempt at definition. The concept, easy enough to grasp in the abstract, is paradoxically more complex and more elusive in concrete application. It is therefore necessary to look more closely at (a) how specified goals are actually stated and (b) under what conditions full attainment or mastery can be said to have occurred. Both of these topics refer to important areas of contemporary educational research and development in the field of assessment. Both are especially pertinent to the development of crediting and certifying systems under lifelong education, as will be elaborated in the final chapter.

Defining Specified Educational Goals

It has already been suggested that a state of full attainment or mastery on the part of a learner makes sense conceptually only in reference to what has been referred to as specified educational goals. If one cannot define the practical limits of some domain of knowledge and performance, then it is always possible that a given learner, no matter how adept already,

might make some sort of qualitatively significant further improvement. The way in which a goal is defined is central to
distinguishing between specified and open educational goals.
The more precisely a goal can be delineated, the more tractable
becomes the problem of ascertaining that the learner has arrived
at a state corresponding to full attainment or mastery. When
full attainment or mastery can be assessed with a reasonable
degree of confidence, crediting and certifying systems that are
independent of the process by which learning took place (e.g.,
formal, non-formal or informal) become feasible. According to
this reasoning the technology for defining specified educational
goals and assessing for mastery represents an essential antecedent to the full implementation of the principles of lifelong education.

Formal Strategies for Specifying Educational Goals

"Learning" is a hypothetical construct used to account for
consistent patterns in behavior. It is not in itself directly
observable, but is inferred from observations of the performance
of learners. If a goal is genuinely specified, it should be
clear exactly what learners will be able to do when the goal has
been fully attained. That is, the definition must be sufficiently inclusive to incorporate *all* relevant learning that may be
manifested in the actions of the learner. When this is achieved,
the concept of full attainment or mastery becomes meaningful.

In order to arrive at a level of specification that makes
it possible to ascertain whether full attainment has been reached, systematic strategies are needed for relating curriculum
content to learner performance. Such strategies are still in
the process of development and testing. But enough progress
has been made for it now to be possible in a practical sense
fully to specify educational goals in many kinds of content
areas. A brief review of progress and possibilities in such
work is needed in order properly to tie down the concept of
specified educational goals.

BEHAVIORAL OBJECTIVES. The simplest and most familiar
strategy for defining specified goals is the behavioral objective, two examples of which were given in the previous chapter.
As formal definitions, objectives must accomplish two things.
They must (a) state the exact conditions and materials available to the learner in the situation in which the learning is
to be assessed and (b) describe concretely the action on the
part of the learner that is indicative of the knowledge or com-

petency in question. Behavioral objectives specify critical
characteristics of assessment situations in reference to domains of educational content. Related tests or other assessment devices are often referred to as "domain-referenced",
whether based on behavioral objectives or on some other formal
specification strategy.

Many proponents of behavioral objectives also insert a
criterion for determining mastery in the objective statement.
While it might seem that mastery would invariably mean perfect
performance, such a high standard would ordinarily be too strin-
gent. Assessment devices are always fallible to some degree,
and even learners who are completely competent with respect to
a given domain may misunderstand an instruction or make a careless error. In any case, the mastery criterion is a separate
conceptual and technical question that has nothing to do with
defining the content domain in behavioral terms.

While behavioral objectives in the form just described and
earlier illustrated have certainly proved themselves to be useful, a number of workers in the field have expressed concern
that the formal definitional strategy from which they are derived may be insufficiently precise. For example, it has been
argued that two individuals working independently from the same
objective might develop assessment devices that are non-parallel
in a psychometric sense. This could occur in the writer's
choice of the format for the assessment tasks, in the interpretation of the exact nature of the action required from the
learner, and in a number of other ways. If the resulting assessment devices differed significantly, then full attainment
or mastery would represent something different on the two tests
or situations. Concern about this possibility has led to the
development of alternative strategies for defining domains of
educational content.

AMPLIFIED BEHAVIORAL OBJECTIVES. In order to further specify the exact nature of learner behaviors representative of the
content domain defined by an objective, Popham (1977) has proposed the "amplified" behavioral objective. This approach combines the standard objective form with a sample assessment task
consistent with the objective plus rules bearing on the nature
of the testing situation, the form of the response alternatives
(if multiple-choice test items are to be developed), and the
way in which responses are to be scored.

The amplified objective is not so much a method for further

defining the content domain as it is a means for providing specific instructions to those who develop the concrete tasks or
test items by which competency in the domain is to be assessed.
A very simple amplified objective developed for illustrative
purposes is shown in Figure 2 following the format in the example provided by Millman (1974).

The illustration in Figure 2 could be supplemented with
further specifications, depending on the sophistication of
those who might be writing the test items. For example, the
level of vocabulary and sentence complexity might also be indicated. However, scrutiny of the specifications listed under
the "amplified objective" heading should reveal that their main
function is to define the nature of the assessment device rather
than to add significantly to the definition of the content domain itself. All of the specifications as well as the original
objective are derived through professional judgment and analysis.
A content domain as defined by an objective is really a kind of
invention, but so is a particular curriculum, instructional
text, or act of teaching. None of this need detract from the
usefulness of either the behavioral objective or its amplified
elaboration.

THE ITEM FORM. An even more precise strategy for defining
educational content domains has been reported by Hively (1973)
and his associates. This approach, developed during the evaluation of an experimental mathematics curriculum, reflects procedures by which Hively transformed objectives stated by curriculum developers into materials for assessing learner outcomes.

In three respects the item form incorporates essential
elements of the amplified objectives just discussed. A general
description of the task is given which approximates a behavioral objective. Specifications are provided for the characteristics of test stimuli and desired learner responses. Scoring
rules are also listed. However, the two new elements incorporated in the item form considerably extend the precision with
which assessment materials can be developed. Formal rules for
generating test items ("item form shells") from sets of test
stimuli ("replacement sets") are included in the item form. In
other words, the complete set of potential test stimuli is provided. Combinations of its various elements are then inserted
into a standard test format according to formal generation
rules, rendering entirely objective the process of developing
assessment tasks consistent with the content domain. No sub-

Objective   Given a sentence in which singular and
                     plural forms of the same verb appear as
                     alternatives, the learner will select
                     that verb form which agrees in number
                     with the subject of the sentence.

Sample Item

   DIRECTIONS   Circle the word in the box that is
                     the correct verb for the sentence.

   EXAMPLE   In winter people to sunny places.

Amplified Objective

Testing Situation

1. Each test item will consist of a simple sentence
   with alternative singular and plural forms of a
   verb that completes the sentence meaningfully.

2. Respondents will be instructed to circle the verb
   form that correctly completes the sentence.

3. Tests constructed from the items will contain an
   equal number of sentences for which singular and
   plural verbs are correct.

Response Alternatives

1. All sentences will be constructed in the present
   tense.

2. The subjects of all sentences must be in the third
   person.

Criterion

Correct responses will be indicated by a circle around the verb
that agrees in number with the subject of the sentence.

FIGURE 2

jective decision or special training is required of the individual developing the assessment materials.

The several examples of item forms given by Hively et al.
(1973) are confined mainly to a mathematics curriculum, and it
may be that this particular approach to developing specified
content domains is useful only in such highly structured content areas. It may also be that the added precision gained by
the use of item forms does not add significantly to the clarity
of interpretation afforded by tests generated from amplified
objectives or even simple behavioral objectives. This is not
the issue here. The item form is of interest as an alternative
illustration of the kind of research and development that is
presently being undertaken to improve the definition and assessment of specified educational goals.

TRANSFORMATION OF INSTRUCTIONAL CONTENT. Related to the
work of Hively and his associates but at the same time striking
out in a new direction is Bormuth's (1970) attempt to derive
evaluation materials directly from instructional content through
the application of principles of linguistics. The examples provided by Bormuth involve the development of formal rules by
which segments of instruction are rearranged in order to obtain
assessment items with certain predetermined characteristics.

Bormuth and to some extent Hively have been especially
concerned that assessment materials be derived directly from
the language of instruction rather than from abstract analyses
of a parent curriculum domain. Bormuth is especially explicit,
even militant, on this point. He strongly objects to contemporary "objectives-based" evaluation systems which provide assessment devices measuring behavioral objectives developed through
structural analyses of generalized domains of curriculum content. Teachers should not be asked to shape instruction so as
to maximize the performance of learners on such objectives,
Bormuth maintains. Rather, the achievement test item should be
tied as closely as possible to instruction by being transformed
directly from instructional language and materials without the
mediation of behavioral objectives and "idiosyncratic" decisions by the developers of assessment devices.

There is an interesting difference of opinion here. Many
educators have maintained for some time that instruction in
schools too often reflects a lack of clear-cut objectives.
Evaluation devices produced by analysis of actual instructional
content in such cases might accurately represent the content of

instruction, yet fail to meet the additional validity criterion of *educational importance* proposed by Cronbach (1969). Still, Anderson (1972) sensibly suggests that in order to know whether or not the learner comprehends actual instruction, it is neces- sary to have "...a system of explicit definitions and rules to derive test items from instructional statements..." (p.149). The utility of approaches utilizing transformational and other grammar should continue to be examined, even if they are limited, as Shoemaker (1975) points out, to instruction formulated entire- ly in the "natural language".

It appears that the transformational approaches are also an alternative means of defining highly specified educational goals. Not only the examples provided by Bormuth, but the very language as well suggests that this is the case, e.g., "...an operational definition of a class of achievement test items is a series of directions which tell an item writer how to rear- range segments of the instruction to obtain items of that type" (p.5). This of course suggests a finite (even if in some cases very large) universe of assessment tasks tied to a clearly spec- ified domain of educational content.

CRITERION SAMPLING. The four strategies for specifying ed- ucational goals and objectives just discussed are particularly pertinent to situations in which the outcomes of systematic learning are being assessed. Each defines a means for moving from the curriculum to precise descriptions of content domains that are behaviorally referenced and amenable to systematic as- sessment. In other words, the four strategies are really pro- cedures for making concrete what it is that learners will be able to do as a result of exposure to a given curriculum.

Where the goal is to assess the competencies of an individ- ual for performing a given type of work, it is inevitable that a wide variety of skills and knowledge, drawn both from formal learning experiences as well as from informal life experiences, will interact in complex ways to account for successful per- formance. In such instances there is usually no single curric- ulum which can be translated through one of the above strategies into specified skills and competencies. Here a different strat- egy for defining the domain of relevant performance is needed.

McClelland (1973) has argued persuasively for a *criterion sampling* approach as the most valid means for defining skills and competencies relating to all types of work. Criterion sam- pling involves analyzing a given job into various elements and

selecting the most critical of the latter for assessment in
situations which are as much like the actual job situation as
possible. This is not different from testing an individual's
ability to drive a car by having that individual actually drive
under conditions that elicit the most important kinds of driving
skills. In this kind of situation the performance domain is already apparent. It does not need to be further delineated
through the application of formal specification strategies.
Rather, assessment instruments and situations are abstracted
directly from an analysis of performance.

McClelland (1973) further advocates that (a) tests based
on criterion samples of job performance should measure skills
that are susceptible to improvement through study or practice;
(b) strategies by which individuals can improve their performance should be made public and explicit; and (c) such tests
should also measure competencies that are involved in clusters
of life outcomes, especially communication skills, the ability
to delay responses (patience), and realistic goal setting. It
goes almost without saying that the criterion sampling approach
and the philosophy which underlies it is highly compatible with
lifelong education. It is in no way tied to attendance at formal learning institutions, focuses on what people can actually
do, and emphasizes open criteria and self-improvement. Certainly the potential of criterion sampling deserves further exploration and application such as that already evidenced in the report by Shavelson, Beckum, and Brown (1974).

Taken together, the five approaches to the delineation of
specified educational goals represent important avenues of research which may greatly facilitate the development of viable
systems for crediting and certifying educational attainment
under lifelong education. It was suggested earlier that without clearly specified domains of achievement and performance,
the concept of full attainment or mastery is meaningless. However, the emerging technical capacity to develop such specifications has served to highlight the need to define mastery itself
more concretely. In particular, conceptually sound decision
rules are needed for establishing at an acceptable level of
certainty whether or not a learner has mastered a domain of education content.

Establishing the Attainment of Mastery

It has already been suggested that perfect performance on
an achievement measure is usually too rigorous a criterion for

establishing mastery. Conversely, there are many situations
in which even perfect performance would not be a certain indicator that an entire content domain has been mastered. The
first aspect of this apparent paradox is attributable to the
familiar concept of error of measurement. Even individuals who
have fully attained a given content domain may not manifest
perfect performance on an assessment device due to carelessness,
distractions, or defects in the instrument itself. The second
part of the paradox reflects the fact that in most cases the
elements which make up evaluation instruments are sampled from
a much larger domain of potential items, tasks, or situations.
Considerations of practicality make it impossible to administer
all of the latter. Therefore, enough items, tasks, or situations must be included on the test or other evaluation device
to attain a reasonable level of confidence that a given learner
can deal successfully with the entire content domain. If an
insufficient number of assessment items is sampled, then even
perfect performance would not be a certain indicator of full
attainment.

The related issues of how many assessment elements should
be sampled for a given domain of content and how many of the
former must be answered correctly in order to conclude with
reasonable assurance that mastery has been attained are conceptual and technical questions of considerable complexity.
Understandably, educational practitioners have not been willing
to wait for the answers. It is common to encounter quite arbitrary rules for determining mastery on tests based on behavioral
objectives or other strategies for defining specified content
domains. There is no obvious rationale, for example, for setting the mastery criterion at eight items correct on a ten-item
test irrespective of whether the items themselves are drawn
from a very small as compared to a very large, even infinite,
set of potential elements.

In the context of a genuinely adaptive instructional situation the use of arbitrary mastery criteria for the formative
evaluation functions of placement and monitoring probably poses
no serious hazards. Such systems should be self-correcting because of their emphasis on regular feedback on the progress of
the learner. Still, conceptually defensible decision rules
would be preferable even here. In the case of the summative
functions of crediting and certifying it is clearly important
that mastery or full attainment be established in a manner that
reduces to a tolerable minimum the possibility of mistaken classification. This is desirable from the point of view of the

learner as well as from that of the society as a whole.

This is not the place to present a technical discussion of ongoing work on the rigorous definition of mastery. Two or three promising lines of work should be cited, however. These approaches all recognize that mastery is a *domain-referenced* concept. That is, interest is focused in the mastery of content domains, not in the mastery of tests or other assessment situations. What is important is a "domain score" rather than a test score. A state of mastery or full attainment in this light is, like learning in general, inferred from performance rather than represented directly by particular sample of performance.

Millman (1973) has approached the problem by using the score on the evaluation instrument as a point estimate of the domain score and applying the binomial theorem to determine the probabilities of correct and incorrect classification of examinees for tests of different lenghts and for different mastery criteria. Harris (1974) has preferred to view mastery in terms of a "sign" rather than a "score" interpretation and has illustrated the relevance of sequential testing procedures for fixed length tests which can be regarded as samples of items from a rigorously defined content domain. Novick and Lewis (1974) applied Bayesian principles to the problem, while Lewis, Wang, and Novick (1973) used the same principles for estimating the proportion of items a given respondent would be likely to answer correctly if the entire content domain were to be administered.

The development of strategies for precisely delineating domains of educational content inevitably introduces the further question of how mastery of those domains is to be recognized once it has been achieved. This is especially the case in the context of lifelong education. Here the relevance of adaptive approaches to the learning/teaching process and the need for systems of crediting and certifying educational attainment on the basis of what learners can do rather than on how their skills were acquired makes assessment for mastery of specified educational goals particularly important.

Conclusion

This chapter has first of all stressed that what are here referred to as specified educational goals are in no way educa-

tionally trivial. Such goals appear to comprise a significant
proportion of the curriculum of schools and to account for a
great many of the skills and competencies that are incorporated
in all types of work, including professional work. Specified
skills and competencies are also building blocks out of which
higher order capacities identified with open-end educational
goals develop. The relationship between these two levels of
learning and development should be seen as interactive and hierarchical.

In order to establish the relevance of specified goals in
the learning/teaching process, it was necessary to present an
analysis of the various formative and summative functions of
L-Evaluation in the classroom or other organized learning situation. It cannot be stressed too strongly that these functions will be differentially utilized depending on the conception of the purpose of schooling that prevails in a given time
and place. Where schooling operates primarily as a selective,
weeding-out process, most evaluation is likely to focus on the
single summative function of selection. Where schooling is
organized to bring virtually all learners up to desired standards of achievement, as would be the case under lifelong education, the other evaluative functions would be extensively utilized. Here the concept of "adaptive" instruction needs to be
introduced, since only a flexible approach to the learning/
teaching process could adequately meet the needs of learners
with widely differing personal characteristics.

A number of current examples of adaptive instruction were
reviewed with the main stress being given to the role of L-
Evaluation. Adopting such a perspective does not induce a
distorted picture, however, as the various regulative functions
of evaluation are intrinsic to all forms of adaptive instruction. Most important, most evaluation under adaptive instruction concerns itself with assessment for full attainment or
mastery of specified educational goals. It is not likely that
this situation would change if other instructional examples had
been chosen, although the particular forms of adaptive instruction that were reviewed should be seen as illustrations rather
than as models to be followed in different contexts.

Finally two areas of research and development essential to
the formation of crediting and certifying systems compatible
with the principles of lifelong education have been appraised.
The first dealt with the formal strategies by which specified
goals are defined. Five such strategies were described, four

of which appear to be especially pertinent to the kinds of knowledge and skills associated with school learning, and the fifth
primarily oriented to the specification of performance skills
associated with employment. All five approaches to the definition of specified goals lead in one way or another to the notion of a rigorously defined domain of content for which it is
at least theoretically possible to ascertain that a given learner has achieved a state of full attainment or mastery.

The second area of research deals directly with the criterion of mastery. In most situations the conclusion that a learner has attained a state of mastery with respect to a given content domain amounts to an inferential statement that is at best
true in a probabilistic sense. Most assessment devices used in
evaluating the attainment of specified goals sample elements
from larger content domains. Since the real interest should be
in the learner's potential performance in the domain rather than
on the test, mathematically tenable rules and strategies are
needed for generalizing from the test to the larger domain of
content.

These two closely related areas of research and development are clearly vital to the functioning of various modes of
adaptive instruction and to the creation of large-scale systems
for crediting and certifying educational achievement. Admittedly
the extensive implementation of principles of adaptive instruction in many societies depends first of all on fundamental
changes in attitudes about the functions of schooling. Basic
changes in attitude are also needed if permanent systems of
crediting and certifying educational attainment outside traditional institutions such as schools are to be accepted. But
so, too, is a tenable conceptual and technical basis for defining specified educational goals and for ascertaining that mastery has been attained. These two ongoing areas of educational
research and development are thus immediately pertinent to the
potential needs of educational systems organized under the principles of lifelong education.

NOTE

1. The designers of the KEDI Instructional System used the
   term "diagnosis" to refer to what is described as "placement" in Table 2. Distinctions between the two terms in
   Table 2 follow Glaser and Nitko (1971), who note that both
   terms have been used by various authorities to describe
   the evaluative function of placement of the learner in the
   instructional sequence. Diagnosis, as used in Table 2,
   refers to assessment for the purpose of determining the
   most appropriate mode of learning for a given learner or
   group of learners. The Korean system does not incorporate
   this particular L-Evaluation function.

CHAPTER 4

OPEN EDUCATIONAL GOALS, EDUCABILITY, AND SELF-DIRECTION

The concept of educability has received increasing attention in recent theoretical work on lifelong education (Dave &
Legrand, 1974; Dave, 1975). Educability refers to a cluster of
learner characteristics that facilitate planful, efficient, and
sustained learning activity. Such patterns of learning presumably reflect the fact that learners are motivated toward self-
improvement, recognize the value of continual learning as a
means of satisfying this motive, possess the skills necessary
for engaging in learning through a variety of modes, and in different settings, and live in a communal and societal context
that provides opportunity for variegated patterns of learning
through their lifetimes.

Educability is a unifying concept for lifelong education.
This is readily inferred from Lebouteux's (1973) report of the
widely prevailing agreement among authorities on lifelong education that schools should be geared primarily to the task of
producing people who are willing and able to plan and carry out
their own later learning activities. In other words, learners
should emerge from schools no longer needing schools. Given
this perspective, the nature of educability itself as well as
its nurture in the environment of the school becomes the fundamental question for evaluation under lifelong education.

The educability concept, because of its very complexity
and inclusiveness, could be a deterrent to the concretization
of the principles of lifelong education into policy and practice.
If educability is to represent everything, then it will have become nothing more than a slogan. This need not be the case,
however. It may be that thinking about the practical realities
of evaluating for educability may help keep a potentially useful
concept from becoming nothing more than a slogan.

Educability is also a most appropriate vehicle for approaching the topic of evaluating the attainment of open educational goals. While it will be evident enough later on that educability has been defined in ways that include both open and specified goals and that also include characteristics of the learner as well as characteristics of institutions and the society, there is no doubt that the concept as articulated thus far places particular stress on the development of certain kinds of open-ended traits in learners, especially those relating to self-direction. But it will also be necessary to look at the context in which learning is to occur. There is a need to explore the characteristics of learning environments that may facilitate the development of learner self-direction.

Educating for Goals that are Open-ended

The distinction between specified and open educational goals is in many respects analogous to the way in which education and training are commonly differentiated. Eisner (1968) makes this familiar distinction as follows:

> The process of education enables individuals to behave intelligently through the exercise of judgment in situations that demand reflection, appraisal, and choice among alternative courses of action. The process of training develops specific types of behavioral responses to specific stimuli or situations. (p.8)

This dichotomy admittedly ignores the continuum lying between the fullest conception of education on the one hand, and training in its most deterministic form on the other. It also ignores the fact that training and education are interactive and mutually reinforcing. Still, like the parallel distinction between specified and open educational goals, the dichotomy is useful. It orients evaluation to different emphases and functions as well as to qualitatively different types of assessment.

Eisner's conception of education calls attention to at least two aspects of human performance. In the first place, to describe an individual's behavior as "intelligent" usually implies that something more than a simple, "correct" response has been observed. Intelligent behavior is associated with the ability to deal with situations that are in some way novel. In such situations there often may be more than one way to solve a problem or accomplish some intention. It is not possible in advance to specify in a concrete manner the exact nature of all correct performance. Any evaluative standards that are formulated must be both general and flexible enough to be applicable to performance that may be original as well as unanticipated. Here attention is focused on educational outcomes that, as Eisner suggests, can be "...appraised only after they emerge." All of the possibilities that might be defined as "intelligent" are not predictable in advance, and intelligence itself may be manifested in different modes and to different degrees.

Secondly, the act of exercising judgment based on reflection, appraisal, and choice evokes the notion of "higher-order" functioning. To judge the desirability of alternatives requires evaluation, the latter standing at the top of the Bloom (1956) taxonomy of cognitive functions. Taken together, the two observations suggest that actions representative of what are thought of as higher-order functions require qualitative assessment rather than a simple determination of whether or not a given response is right or wrong. In fact, viewing such higher-order performance as simply a reaction to a set of external stimulus conditions ignores their essential character. Regarding all human behavior as merely a response to some environmental stimulus belies the nature of much higher-order performance, especially when it is of a productive nature. The outcomes of creative activity such as a painting or a theoretical insight in science cannot be meaningfully interpreted or understood as simple "responses."

The brief introduction to open-ended goals in Chapter 2 made it clear that the concept should not be associated solely with characteristics of learners. Structural and organizational principles of education can also be open-ended, as was illustrated for the lifelong educational principle of Horizontal Integration. Likewise, the learning/teaching process itself can be defined in terms of open-ended objectives. In general, with movement towards educational outcomes that are summative, inclusive, and distal in their consequences, it is impossible to avoid confronting educational goals of the open variety.

Three Kinds of Open Educational Goals

There are at least three kinds of open educational goals, all of them represented in the criteria for lifelong education discussed in the first chapter. In fact, all of the criterion statements listed in that chapter refer to open goals. Each describes states, conditions, or activities for which full attainment cannot be defined. All appear to imply the possibility

of alternative modes of achievement. All suggest the appropriateness of qualitative scales of evaluation. All appear to
have a "higher-order" character in being the complex product of
many interacting elements or structures. These three types of
open goals may be labeled as *situational*, *structural*, and *learner*. These refer, respectively, to goals associated with the
situation in which learning takes place, to the ways in which
educational institutions and systems are organized, and to outcomes in learners themselves.

     OPEN GOALS - SITUATIONAL. The distinction between open
and closed educational goals when applied to the learning situation implies that at least some situations are arranged so as
to encourage diversity of outcomes. This kind of learning context has been identified by Eisner (1968) with the concept of
"expressive" objectives.

> An expressive objective describes an educational en-
> counter: it identifies a situation in which children
> are to work, a problem with which they are to cope,
> a task in which they are to engage; but it does not
> specify what from that encounter, situation, problem,
> or task they are to learn. (p.15)

     The expressive objective is formulated to promote diversity
rather than homogeneity of performance. It differs from the behavioral objective associated with specified goals in the essential respect of allowing, even encouraging, solutions or prod-
ucts that are unusual and perhaps even unique. It applies to
situations in which it is not possible to predict all of the
potential outcomes. However, the identification of expressive
objectives with high-level outcomes of education does not argue
for the triviality of specified goals. The interaction between
accomplishments reflecting the two types of goals is clearly
recognized in Eisner's distinction between instructional (read
"behavioral") and expressive objectives:

> Instructional objectives embody the codes and the skills
> that culture has to provide and which make inquiry pos-
> sible. Expressive objectives designate those circum-
> stances in which the codes and the skills acquired in
> instructional contexts can be used and elaborated...
> (p.17)

     While open as to outcomes, an expressive situational ob-
jective may be quite precise about the nature of the conditions
which should comprise the learning context. For example, detail-

ed and comprehensive models of teaching might be developed for
the purpose of creating and maintaining contexts which facilitate learning of the open variety. Several of the models described in Joyce and Weil's (1972) *Models of Teaching* appear to
be directed primarily to the pursuit of open outcomes. Perhaps
the first known model of teaching for open goals was developed
a very long time ago in the form of what has come to be known
as the "Socratic method."

Models of teaching and learning directed at the attainment
of open outcomes are in a sense highly elaborated expressive
objectives. Teaching or learning models define the situation
under which learning is to occur. In its simplest form an expressive objective amounts to little more than a description of
a certain type of task. Eisner's examples of expressive objectives describe tasks rather than situations or circumstances.
"To interpret the meaning of *Paradise Lost*," or "to develop a
three-dimensional form through the use of wire and wood," are
definitions of tasks rather than learning situations. Still,
such tasks would be most appropriately undertaken in contexts
structured so as to encourage individuals to approach the problem in their own way. When Eisner suggested that the most so-
phisticated forms of intellectual work (such as those which
occur in the artist's studio, the research laboratory, or the
graduate seminar) place greater emphasis on expressive rather
than instructional objectives, he of course had in mind what
are here referred to as open learning contexts.

What function does evaluation play in such open situations?
Learning situations are designed in order to establish and maintain *conditions* that facilitate certain types of learning. Here
C-Evaluation, both formative and summative, is relevant. In the
case of formative evaluation, the obvious need would be to determine to what extent there is *congruence* between intended and
actual circumstances and conditions. That is, formative evaluation would provide information concerning how closely the actual
learning situation corresponds to the ideal situation as defined
in the expressive objective, teaching model, etc. Here evaluation deals with the educational process. It acts to promote and
maintain a desirable set of conditions and circumstances. In
contrast, summative evaluation focuses on the same conditions
and circumstances, but is conducted in order to draw conclusions
that have an element of finality. Summative evaluation asks
whether or not a total effort has been successful in the special
sense of whether the desired conditions and processes have been
established and maintained over time. The kinds of phenomena

measured and observed are all associated with the learning context rather than with learning itself.

A related question naturally has to do with what open learning situations might be like. Illustrative thought and research on this topic will be described later, after the remaining two kinds of open educational goals have been described.

OPEN GOALS - STRUCTURAL. One of the significant characteristics of the evaluative criteria for lifelong education summarized in the first chapter is the very strong emphasis given to the way in which educational systems and institutions should be organized. The principles of integration and articulation can be generalized to any level, including the learning group as well as the individual learner. But there is embedded in thought about lifelong education an awareness of the fact that impact at the micro level is not likely to be significant unless institutions and broader social systems are organized in ways consistent with the principles that are to operate in the learning situation itself.

Organizational and structural goals associated with lifelong education define open ends. An ideal state of integration among educational delivery systems is conceivable only in abstract terms. There are no rules for deciding when optimal organizational integration has been achieved. There are undoubtedly a variety of models on which successful integration might be based. As in the case of the concept of "intelligent" behavior discussed above, evaluative criteria must reflect a position along a dimension of quality rather than be absolutely attained or unattained.

Accessibility is without doubt the most fundamental theme in structural and organizational principles of lifelong education. Institutions and the systems in which they are incorporated are to make education and training at all levels open to all who need and want it. Even the parallel principle of *variety* - that diverse means should be available for engaging in a given type of education or training - is really another facet of accessibility. Educational opportunity is fully accessible only if it is available in a form and at a place that is appropriate for all classes of potential learners.

In view of the importance of the accessibility theme, it is obvious that utilization of educational alternatives constitutes the final criterion for evaluating attempts to implement structural and organizational goals. But utilization would be a very complex indicator at the macro level of institution and system. If, for example, the educational systems of a country were organized so as to allow individuals to move by various paths through formal, non-formal, and informal education modes, then the extent to which the various paths are used would be perhaps more important than the frequency with which each mode by itself is selected. If a given path were rarely or never chosen or, if chosen, never completed, then something would clearly be amiss.

The variety of organizational and structural possibilities under a well-articulated concept of lifelong education is impressive. Spaulding (1974) elaborates the formal, non-formal, and informal trichotomy into six distinct kinds of educational services:

1. Highly structured institutions with prescriptive programs such as characterize most schools and universities;

2. Equally structured institutions which have enough flexibility in their programs to allow for a choice among alternatives such as alternative schools, multi-unit schools, and modern comprehensive schools;

3. Moderately structured institutions offering formal courses aimed at prescriptive learning goals, including correspondence courses, work-study arrangements, self-learning centers, and community centers;

4. Loosely structured services that seek to inform and influence target audiences about prescriptive content domains including consumer and health education agencies, agricultural information services, and various kinds of job training;

5. Groups governed by voluntary participants such as youth organizations, political organizations, interest groups, and societies providing voluntary service; and

6. Informal and educational media, including television, radio, print media, libraries, and bookstores.

Under the concept of utilization adopted here, all of
Spaulding's six types of educational delivery systems could be
extensively used in a society, and yet such presumably favorable
statistics could mask still a serious lack of integration within, as well as articulation between, various levels of the educational spectrum. This is commonly manifested in many modern
societies, both developed and less developed, in the resistance
of formal institutions in categories (1) and (2) to recognize
and credit learning accomplished by means of one of the other
four systems of delivery. Spaulding has also stressed the vital
importance of effective crediting systems for non-formal and
informal education. He does so in spite of his recognition of
the potentially dangerous implications of excessive governmental
record-keeping on individual citizens.

While popular use of educational options may be the final
criterion in the case of structural goals, organizational and
other models are just as relevant here as are teaching and learning models in the learning situation. Such models, based on
theories derived from the principles of lifelong education,
could provide standards against which present reality may be
judged. Likewise, both formative and summative evaluation have
their place, although the time dimension for the former is much
longer than in the learning situation. If the purpose of the
evaluation is to shape the implementation of certain kinds of
structures for institutions and systems, then the evaluation is
clearly formative. If the purpose is one of rendering a summary judgment on the structure as to adoption (or discontinua-
tion) then the evaluation is summative.

At the macro level of institution and system, decision
making in education is only partially influenced by objective
information on effectiveness and congruency with models. Evaluation must also take into account potent political factors.
Programs can be shown to be effective in terms of their own
goals, yet be discontinued because they are unpopular. Other
programs may be continued for political reasons even though
evaluative findings show them to be relatively ineffective in
terms of stated program goals. The latter was the case for the
Head Start program for educationally disadvantaged pre-school
children in the USA (Evans and Williams, 1972). But evaluations,
especially those that scrutinize institutions and systems, are
naively limited in scope and effectiveness if they do not assess
attitudes, preferences, and motivations that underlie political
forces. Such variables are the legitimate concern of evaluation
and this is particularly true at the macro level.

OPEN GOALS - LEARNER. Virtually all contemporary thought dealing with educational goals and objectives for learners articulates in one way or another some sort of concept of open-ended objectives. Gagné (1964) perhaps does not make this explicit in his analysis of learning hierarchies, although he does refer to the need for learners to *discover* rules in order to formulate "higher-order principles" that form the basis of problem-solving strategies.

It has been noted that Cronbach (1971a) used the term "open-ended" to describe "intelligent analysis and problem-solving" as well as "creative and self-expressive production." Bloom (1956), in the taxonomy of educational objectives (cognitive), did not explicitly deal with the specified versus open distinction. However, evaluation, the highest of the six levels of the taxonomy, was not viewed as a final step in thinking or problem solving. Bloom and his associates suggest: "It is quite possible that the evaluative process will in some cases be the prelude to the acquisition of new knowledge, a new attempt at comprehension or application, or a new analysis and synthesis" (p.185).

Evaluation in the taxonomy refers to the application of either internal or external standards to ideas, works, or solutions. Viable standards are based on knowledge of the domain in question. This is precisely what aesthetic criticism involves, as Eisner (1968) points out. In literary or artistic criticism, work and performances are not evaluated in terms of their similarity to an exemplary model. They are unique events to which evaluative criteria are applied through systematic judgment and appraisal. The initial rejection of new forms and practices in art can often be traced in retrospect to the application by critics of evaluative criteria that were appropriate for earlier conceptions of a medium. This does not mean that standards change so radically that everything that is new will later by widely accepted as excellent, or that every criticism of something new must be based on standards that will soon become obsolete. It does imply that evaluative standards for open-ended performance domains must be formulated so as to address instances that have not yet been observed and that are not entirely predictable.

Cautions

Earlier work on the measurement of "divergent" thinking anticipates many of the measurement issues that will be encountered in evaluating for open goals. Guilford's (1967) concept of divergent thinking deals with situations in which diverse patterns of thought and action are both likely and appropriate. In contrast, specified goals have been identified with convergent content requiring single correct answers. Recognition and recall are often sufficient to assess the attainment of specified goals. Assessment devices and situations used to measure the attainment of specified goals often require the learner merely to select the correct answer. But divergent performance often means that the learner has produced something - a solution to a problem, a design, or a conception. Devices for assessing divergent thinking may mimic in form the activities on which they were modeled. Respondents are asked to think of original titles to brief stories, to find new uses for common objects, or to predict possible consequences of certain kinds of events.

Evaluation when confronting open goals must take a radically different stance concerning the kinds of conclusions that may be drawn about learners. Crediting and certifying in terms of *mastery* are justifiable and practicable only where a goal can be concretely specified and communicated to learners and teachers. Excellence of accomplishment in domains defined by open goals can be assessed and recognized. But even excellence does not imply mastery.

It is of course possible to limit open domains of performance artificially by means of standards or criteria specifying that a particular level of performance is good enough for a given purpose. This was illustrated in Chapter 2 in the brief discussion of an arbitrary criterion for successful performance on the *Unusual Uses* test. But establishing an arbitrary criterion does not change the real nature of an open domain nor is it in any way equivalent to a true mastery interpretation. Such standards provided information about the learner's level of competence in the content domain and in that sense are domain-referenced interpretations. But the standard itself is invariably interpreted in terms of how well others perform. For example, even a direct performance measure such as typing speed (words per minute with a minimum frequency of errors) is primarily meaningful in reference to the speed of typists in general. If 90% of the available typists could type no more than 30 words per minute, then a typist who could manage 35 or 40 words per minute would be fast.

Mastery as *full* attainment cannot be defined in the case of typing just as it cannot be defined for an athlete running

the 1,500 meters. In the case of an open cognitive domain such
as reading comprehension, the level of complexity of reading
passages used and the difficulty of the task itself (e.g., merely reporting factual information from the passage as opposed to
drawing valid inferences from that passage) can be established
in a manner that lends itself to the setting of standards with
no implication that mastery will be assessed. A portion of an
open domain has merely been delimited for a specific purpose
without altering the fundamental nature of the domain itself.

The inappropriate use of measures of open-ended goals as
crediting and certifying devices could contaminate a deliberately democratized system for evaluating learners by reintroducing
the very elitism and selectivity that it was designed to eliminate. The performance of learners on many kinds of open-ended
goals and objectives may be influenced by factors that are not
traceable to education per se. The educational level of the
family, the learner's role, ethnicity, and even heredity may in
part influence these kinds of accomplishments. Formative and
summative evaluation in the learning situation are relevant,
just as with goals of the specified variety. But the characteristics being evaluated (the most important open goals) are not
concrete skills and competencies. Rather, they usually reflect
capacities and potentialities. True, society attempts through
education to nurture capacities and potentials whose limits in
human performance may remain unspecified and whose origins are
not completely ascribable to purely educational influences. But
standards set for crediting and certifying performance in these
areas can never imply mastery.

The democratization principle of lifelong education has had
a major influence on the conception of evaluation presented in
these pages. The crediting and certifying functions of the pre-
ceding chapter are meant to supplant much of the contemporary
emphasis on evaluation for selective purposes. But typical *selection* devices usually measure open-ended goals reflecting generalized potential rather than what individuals can actually do
or perform. In the perspective on evaluation taken here, open
ended goals, especially at the level of the learner, are of
great importance. But measures of such goals must not be used
to establish mastery in the crediting and certifying process if
the latter is to reflect solely accomplishment that is attributable to the deliberate outcomes of education, whether formal,
non-formal, or even informal. Measures of open-ended goals
should only be used for these evaluative functions when performance is interpreted in terms of fair and relevant criteria or

standards referenced directly to acceptable levels of competence in various social and work roles.

Defining Open-ended Goals in Ways that Relate to Educational Practice

The question of how open-ended goals are to be defined is just as significant as was the same question in the case of specified goals. Without careful definition of what is to be measured, valid assessment is highly improbable. Without valid assessment, evaluation is stranded without a reality-base. Constructing definitions that bridge the gap between words and action is a vital step in bringing about educational change. In the case of lifelong education this transition is especially critical where the intention is to shape educational practice in the direction of fostering open-ended goals associated with educability in learners.

Definition strategies for specified and open goals are polar opposites in terms of the ways in which they can be mis-applied. With specified goals, the strategies for definition reviewed in the last chapter, if carried to extremes of speci-ficity, can multiply the number of objectives excessively. In contrast, open-ended goal definitions, unless rigorously thought out, may become so inclusive as to subsume nearly everything that is good, while obscuring meaningful differentiations among varieties of educational outcomes. It has been noted that this is a potential danger in the case of the educability concept.

A satisfactory definition of an open-ended educational goal anticipates and eliminates confusing *non-instances* of the goal. That is, the definition not only describes the kinds of perfor-mances that are representative of the goal, but also cites re-lated performances that are not representative. Excellent il-lustrations of this process are contained in Cronbach's (1971b) discussion of test validation.

Cronbach refers to reading comprehension in his first ex-ample. It is possible to formulate rough standards as to when the reading comprehension skills of a given learner are suffi-cient for a particular purpose, but it is not possible to define some level of reading comprehension beyond which further improve-ment may not occur. The reason for this is that the textual ma-terial on which reading comprehension performance is assessed can always be made more difficult within the parameters avail-able in a given language.

Consider Cronbach's single sentence definition of reading comprehension:

> The student considered superior in reading comprehension is one who, if acquainted with the words in a paragraph, will be able to derive from the paragraph the same conclusions that other educated readers, previously uninformed on the subject of the paragraph, derive. (p.463)

The nature of reading comprehension is reasonably clear. The person being tested must derive accurate conclusions from a reading passage. (A more elaborate definition would of course indicate what is meant by "derive...conclusions," but this simple example is quite useful as an illustration.) The rest of the definition indicates what reading comprehension is *not*. Specifically, it is not size of vocabulary, reading speed, or level of information. How is it possible to know this? The definition indicates that readers are assumed to be educated, and we know that vocabulary is highly correlated with educational level. All examinees should have a sufficient level of education to justify the assumption that the words in the passage are familiar. If this assumption is not met, the test is invalid for the group in question because the results will be influenced by knowledge of vocabulary in addition to reading comprehension skills. Likewise, the definition does not mention a time limit for reading a passage, so that it can be concluded that reading speed is not to be confused with reading comprehension. Finally, the passage is to be on a subject on which all examinees are likely to be ignorant. Questions cannot be answered on the basis of general information previously acquired.

In Cronbach's example, vocabulary, reading speed, and information all represent "counterhypotheses" that have been deliberately eliminated in the definition. In the language of assessment theory "reading comprehension" is a *construct*. Counterhypotheses, by stating what is *not* meant by a construct, operate to delimit the domain of relevant performance by distinguishing it from other, related domains. By these means constructs are prevented from being overly inclusive and as a result meaningless.

It should be clear that all open-ended educational goals refer to possible constructs, whether stated at the level of the learner, the learning situation, or the organization or

system set up to promote learning. Horizontal integration between home and school is thus a potential construct. To be
measurable in a valid way it must be clear both what it is, and
what it is not. Not every relationship between home and school
is likely to be indicative of horizontal integration. For example, one-way relationships, such as when the school sends a
report to the parent on a child's academic performance, do not
necessarily imply integration according to the principles stated
in the first chapter. Likewise, "self-understanding," "self-
evaluation," and "inter-learning" all refer to possible constructs that are as yet undefined or at best only partially
defined. On the other hand, "individualization of learning" is
a situational construct, one for which a number of definitions
and associated practices already exist. All of these terms
refer to open-ended educational goals that could assume construct status when suitably defined.

Transforming goals into constructs is a necessary first
step if valid educational instruments and procedures are to be
constructed. But even precisely stated constructs are in themselves insufficient guides for the development of educational
practice and associated evaluation strategies. Linkages need
to be built between learner and situational constructs, and between the latter and structural constructs. In the first case,
this means that an effective evaluation practice must assess
both the learner and the situation in which learning occurs,
especially the educational practices that are embedded in that
situation.

Generally speaking, education is not blessed with a vali-
dated arsenal of praxes guaranteed to produce various kinds of
desirable outcomes in learners. It would be wrong to pretend
that an established science of teaching and learning will invariably produce what is wanted in the majority of learners.
If this is true for basic curriculum domains defined by specified goals, then it is true many times over for aspects of the
curriculum that incorporate open-ended goals associated with
the concept of educability. Not only is there uncertainty
about how to facilitate the development in learners of relevant
characteristics, there is equal uncertainty about how to recognize such development when it occurs. How, then, is it possible to move from rhetoric to practice (both instructional and
evaluative) in the face of such uncertainties?

The gap between abstract goals and practice can be effectively bridged only through systematic conception and analysis.

In its turn, evaluation cannot be conceived without constructs that define what is to be measured and without a conception of what practice is supposed to be like. Progress in evaluation follows the development of clearly defined learning constructs and related practices.

There appear to be four steps involved in the conception and analysis just referred to. These consist of (a) the elaboration of open-ended goals at the level of the learner into what have been referred to here as theoretical constructs, followed by (b) the deduction of relevant instructional principles from the constructs, leading to (c) organization of the instructional principles into an instructional theory, and finally (d) application of the theory to the development of one or more instructional models that in turn lead to concrete instructional practices. As a series of prescriptive steps, these stages are:

State goals as theoretical constructs

Deduce principles of educational practice from constructs

Combine principles into a theory about instruction

Apply theory to the development of practice

This series of steps is not always easy to carry out, but it does lead from ideas to application. The following is an elaboration of a brief section of the report by Skager and Dave (1977). It is based on an actual conceptual interchange about participants in the multinational curriculum evaluation project summarized in that document, and illustrates how constructs can be applied to personality characteristics as well as to domains of educational content.

During a discussion of an aspect of the educability concept having to do with the learner's view of the self, it was evident that three somewhat different goals were being used in approximately the same context. First, it was seen as essential that learners be "self-aware," especially in regard to the quality and results of their own performance. Self-awareness would presumably imply the ability to evaluate one's own performance. But it was felt to be equally important that learners possess an appropriate degree of "self-confidence." Without self-confidence individuals might be unwilling to attempt to learn, especially in situations requiring independence and self-direction. Finally, a long-term goal of education was seen as "self-acceptance," or the ability to place value on the self as it really is. Without self-acceptance and concomitant self-valuing there might be little motivation to engage in activities that would lead to self-improvement, nor little realism exercised in the nature of the activities selected. Were the real self not acceptable, it was reasoned, constructive efforts at self-improvement through education might not be perceived to be worthwhile. Self-neglectful or even self-destructive behavior could be the more probably outcome.

The above are merely hypotheses. But they are reasonably plausible hypotheses, and plausible hypotheses are the source from which educational practice usually develops. But in the discussion just referred to, clarification of the nature of, and relation between, the three goals of self-awareness, self-confidence, and self-acceptance was definitely needed. All three concepts as educational goals appeared to be important in the discussion, but their specific referents needed to be delineated as well as their relation to one another and to possibly relevant educational practices.

Such delineation begins with the development of constructs, or so it is suggested above. Constructs are inventions. They are not given by nature, but are invented in order to explain what has been observed to occur in nature as well as to predict what might occur under various sets of circumstances. The following are a rendering of the constructs that appeared to be developing in the discussion alluded to above.

> *Self-Awareness* refers to a state in which the learner manifests knowledge about the quality or adequacy of his or her own performance with respect to a defined or specified domain of educational content that is in substantial agreement with an independent assessment of that same performance by an individual qualified through competence and objectivity to make such an assessment.

Self-awareness as used here refers strictly and solely to evaluative information learners possess about their performance *qua* learners. It is especially important to note the variety of alternative interpretations of self-awareness that are specifically disallowed under the definition.

1. The construct does not refer to generalized knowledge about the self. It is confined to performance

in purposeful learning situations.

2. The construct does not apply to learning as a
   whole, but rather to clearly defined or specified
   domains of educational content. Self-awareness,
   at least as used in the theory being developed
   here, is domain specific.

3. Self-awareness does not imply that the evaluation
   is done by learners themselves. This may be the
   case, but it is equally possible that the learner
   may have absorbed an evaluation made by an external
   agent. The construct refers only to a state of
   awareness, not to the process of self-evaluation.

4. Self-awareness does not mean merely that the learner can give an opinion as to how well he or she has
   performed, but that such an opinion will be verified
   by an independent authority.

"Self-awareness," until elaborated as a construct, is merely a descriptive term in the ordinary language. It can be defined in a variety of ways. Others might wish to give it a far
more general meaning than has been assigned here. This does not
imply that some sort of debate should be undertaken in order to
arrive at a single meaning for the term. The above definition
provides reasonably specific guidance as to what an evaluative
instrument developed to measure self-awareness should tell in
terms of the particular theory being developed here.

> *Self-confidence* refers to an accurate perception on
> the part of the learner of personal competence to
> deal successfully with tasks, problems, or situations
> representative of some domain or educational content
> (specified or open) that is familiar.

Self-confidence according to this definition refers to the
learner's prediction that his or her own future performance
will be successful. This suggests various approaches to assessment which would have learners predict their own levels of performance in situations representative of given domains of content. Like self-awareness, this construct excludes situations
other than those that incorporate purposeful learning activity.
It is also content domain specific. Alternative connotations
of the notion of self-confidence excluded in this particular
construct include:

1. Self-confidence as defined above must be realistic. The term "accurate" means that the learner's predictions are to be verified in actual
   performance with the task, problem, or situation.
   Mere expression of self-confidence followed by
   subsequent failure is not an instance of the
   construct.

2. Self-confidence refers to future, rather than
   present, performance. If it referred to the
   latter it would be indistinguishable from the
   previous construct of self-awareness.

3. Self-confidence implies some sort of familiarity
   with the domain in question. A prediction of
   success could be nothing more than the posturing
   of a gambler and, as such, could represent merely
   a generalized trait of self-confidence across
   many situations regardless of learners' knowledge-
   ability about their own competencies. In this
   sense the self-awareness is to be seen as preced-
   ing self-confidence developmentally.

Taken together, the first two constructs relate in a hierarchical way. Both are derived from experience with a domain
of educational content, but self-confidence is based on a particular type of self-awareness, e.g., a history of successful
performance in that domain.

Self-Acceptance is a positive assessment of the self
as competent in the role of a learner that is generalized over a significant variety of learning domains
and situations and that is based on a personal history
of successful performance.

Self-acceptance is generalized confidence in the self as a
learner. It is a willingness to say, "Based on what I know
about my own past performance, I am competent to engage successfully in learning activities in a variety of domains and situations." Self-acceptance, like the other two constructs, is restricted to purposeful learning activities, although it adds
the idea of different learning situations. But what is excluded
in the definition?

1. Self-acceptance does not imply that the learner
   feels competent to deal with *all* learning situa-

tions or all content domains. The construct merely suggests that there must be a significant degree
of generalization of the learner's confidence in
the self as a learner across domains and situations.
A self-accepting learner would still be able to say,
"I have no trouble learning languages, although admittedly I have always been hopeless in mathematics."
Likewise, another self-accepting learner might admit
that, "I was always at the bottom of the class in
school, but I learned what I needed to know on my
own once I perceived its relevance to my own future."
In other words, self-acceptance must be realistic
and differentiated. People who see themselves as
competent in all learning domains are more likely to
be suffering from delusions than they are likely to
be individuals of rare genius.

2. Self-acceptance is a generalized attitude based on
   a relatively long personal history as a learner.
   It does not imply merely feeling that one could be
   successful if one had to be, but also requires a
   record of accomplishment that can only be amassed
   over time. Because the construct incorporates the
   notion of persistence over time, verification of
   the reality basis of self-acceptance requires an
   examination of the record of actual achievement.

Taken together, the three constructs form a hierarchy growing out of experience acquired in purposeful learning. Each
construct also suggests a basic approach to assessment and as
a result would lead to the development of evaluative instruments.
With the constructs now defined, the first of the four steps
leading from educational goals to instructional practice has
been taken. The other three steps are summarized in the figure.
Here the relationships among the constructs is displayed and
their origin in the learner's experience is stated as a set of
postulates. A relevant theory of instruction is derived from
the postulates. Finally, related instructional models are
listed.

The instructional theory displayed in the figure is properly classified as a "common-sense" theory. It has been developed
for purposes of illustration rather than as an exhaustive treatment of an important aspect of the concept of educability. Related (and more elaborate) theories are to be found in the literature on the self-concept (see, for example, Shavelson, Hubner,

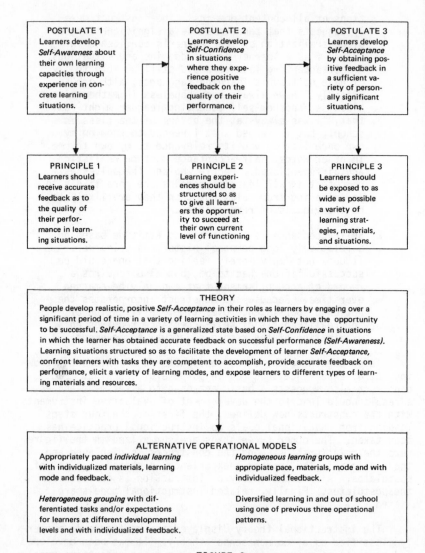

FIGURE 3

ILLUSTRATIVE CONSTRUCT-THEORY-PRACTICE LINKAGE (CTPL)
FOR SELF-ACCEPTANCE IN LEARNERS

& Stanton, 1976). But the theory seems sensible. It leads
rather naturally to a variety of instructional models and associated practices, all of which incidentally are compatible
with the general notion of adaptive instruction presented in
the last chapter.

The separate constructs do not lead to different instructional models. Interrelationships among them as well as the
holistic nature of instruction itself mean that all instructional models consistent with the theory must contain three critical
elements: (a) feedback to the learner on the quality of his or
her performance, (b) the opportunity to be successful, and (c)
the opportunity to experience a variety of learning contexts
and situations.

These elements in turn suggest evaluative criteria referenced to the situation in which learning takes place (C-Evaluation), just as the construct definitions developed initially
refer to relevant characteristics of learners (L-Evaluation).
In order to proceed with evaluation itself, a variety of types
of assessment procedures could (and should) be developed to
measure both situational and learner characteristics. However,
the critical question of what is to be assessed in the evaluation is answered through the theoretical linkage between constructs defining open educational goals at the level of the
learner and deduced educational practices designed to enhance
the development of such characteristics in learners.

Having examined one example of a conceptual and analytical
process leading from open educational goals to real educational
practice, it is time to confront the critical concept of educability. The discussion that follows is only an early step in
the elucidation of the concept. Its purpose is to examine some
of the conceptual and evidential base for educability as well
as to anticipate the kinds of constructs that are likely to
devolve from it, both with respect to the characteristics of
learners themselves and to the nature of the situation in which
learning takes place.

Evaluating for Educability

At its core, the concept of learner educability incorporates the principle that human beings make choices. Educability
not only implies that an individual *can* learn, it implies that
the individual will *choose* to learn and will also be able to

choose the time, manner, and place and content of learning. Inherent in the idea of choice is the assumption that individuals can learn to set their own goals, that goal-seeking behavior is just as important as goal-attaining behavior. As March (1972) has suggested, "Human choice behavior is at least as much a process of discovering goals as of acting on them" (p.420).

Contemporary evaluation models appear to be entirely concerned with goal-attaining behavior rather than with goal-seeking behavior. On the one hand March posits a "theory of childhood" emphasizing opportunity for choosing as a way of enlarging the child's perspective of the world. As adults "...we try to lead the child to do things that are inconsistent with his present goal because we know (or believe) that he can only develop into an interesting person by coming to appreciate aspects of experience that he initially rejects" (March, 1972, p. 421). The contrasting "theory of adulthood," on the other hand, is intensely rationalist. Choice becomes the consequence of pre-existing intention. Models of evaluation are similarly limited to situations in which goals have already been determined (and are not themselves subject to evaluation), and the task is one of assessing the congruency between outcomes and specific objectives derived from the goals.

March (1972) further notes that this somewhat invidious comparison between children and adults leads many well-meaning and liberal individuals to apply the adult model to childhood by assuming that children already have somehow fully determined their own goals and all that is needed is a completely unrestricted environment (especially in the school) in which children can freely set about attaining these goals. This view must be in error unless the assumption is to be made that personal goals are set independently of the individual's interactions with the environment. Rather, March (1972) turns the tables and suggests that a far more productive tactic would be to apply the childhood model to adults. Even adults should be ready to engage in a process of developing "more interesting 'wants'."

The above suggests two fundamental principles that should guide thinking about evaluation for educability. First, goal-seeking behavior as manifested in curiosity, exploration, and even playfulness is just as important as behavior that reflects systematic attempts to attain a predetermined goal. This can lead to radically different perceptions of the value of many kinds of learner activities. For example, March's thinking suggests that imitation, so characteristic of both play and purposeful learning in children, instead of being a rather primitive learning strategy, may in many contexts actually represent goal seeking. The learner is really experimenting with different social roles and activities. Likewise, playfulness, so non-productive in the rationalistic view of adult learning, would be seen under the alternative view as a way of experimenting with reality. Many forms of play, rather than being mere entertainment, may in reality be exploratory behavior that incorporates goal seeking. According to this analysis the avoidance of exploratory, whimsical, or fantasizing play among adults in many societies may reflect a social context that suppresses this basic aspect of educability. The typical play activities of adults in organized games under formal rule structures can hardly be characterized as "exploratory."

Secondly, application of March's "childhood model" to evaluation practice suggests that under certain circumstances it is not appropriate to specify criteria in advance, except perhaps at a relatively abstract and qualitative level. Since it is impossible to predict exactly what will emerge from exploratory, goal-setting behavior, it may often be unwise to specify that only certain outcomes will be taken as evidence that an educational experience has been successful for a given individual. In evaluation, as in the rest of life, the criteria adopted determine what will be observed. It is important that real goal-seeking behavior goes on and that it eventually gets somewhere. But it is probably wiser from the perspective of evaluation to allow goal-seeking behavior to run its course, since new criteria may have to be applied that would not have been thought of in advance. Macdonald (1974) suggests that,

> ...we may encourage students to play with ideas or materials with the intent of providing the experience of flexibility and to encourage a creative response to phenomena. Or we may ask students to explore systematically through observation and manipulation *without predetermining the end of this experience*. (p.10 italics mine)

It should be clear that an evaluation practice which focuses solely on what Macdonald refers to as the "objectified outcomes of the learning process" is massively misapplied to the kind of exploratory, goal-setting activity that appears to be so basic to the concept of educability. This type of evaluation does have an important place, or the previous chapter

would not have been written. But there are also times when the
imposition of objectified, prespecified outcomes is potentially
self-defeating. The nature of an appropriate alternative strategy for evaluation would emphasize observation of "...the activity of the student *in* the learning process, not the restricted
and objectified outcomes of this process" (Macdonald, p.12).

These are thus two fundamental principles. The first as-
serts the centrality of goal-setting behavior to the educability
concept. The second calls for an evaluation practice that
avoids the imposition of gratuitous, prespecified outcomes in
the face of potentially productive exploratory behavior. It is
now appropriate to examine educability in terms of (a) the kinds
of constructs about individuals that are implied by the concept
and (b) the possible nature of learning situations designed to
facilitate its development.

Educability and the Self-Directed Learner

Dave (1973) has elaborated the concept of educability in
terms of five kinds of learner characteristics:

1. The ability to utilize different learning strategies, such as working independently or co-operatively in groups;

2. Competency in basic learning skills such as purposeful reading, observing, listening, comprehension, and communication;

3. Developed intellectual skills such as reasoning,
   critical thinking, and organizing and application;

4. Ability to use various learning media including
   textbooks, periodicals, and programmed aides;

5. Ability to organize one's own learning experiences
   through identification of needs, planning and carrying out learning activities, and evaluating one's
   own accomplishments.

Dave's conception of educability includes all personal
characteristics that have a significant bearing on how an individual learns. Yet surprisingly, the first four of his five
clusters do not appear to be beyond the reach of the best contemporary pedagogy. It is possible to teach most children to

read, listen, observe, etc., if they can be got to attend school long enough. Given the necessary resources, it would not be difficult to set up educational programs designed to expose learners to a variety of learning modes and instructional media. True, there is often a decision not to do so, or the resources may be lacking. All societies could no doubt do a better job of developing the first four kinds of competencies and capacities in the majority of their citizens. But beyond resources and commitment there seems to be nothing really intractable about the first four clusters of the educability concept, nothing at least that most educators would not feel they could accomplish for the great majority of learners given sufficient time and favorable conditions. Unfortunately, in the case of the critical fifth cluster the situation is radically different. Individuals who can set their own goals, plan and carry out their own learning, and evaluate the results are *self-directed* learners.

There is already a general recognition of the importance of self-direction in learning, above all in the literature of lifelong education. But great controversy and uncertainty exists as to how development of such self-direction may be fostered. As an institution which guides and controls the learning process, the school is seen by many as utterly hostile to the development of learner self-direction, so much so that Illich (1971) and others even propose that society "deschool" itself. Other writers maintain that institutionalized learning environments such as the school can be organized so as to promote self-direction in learners, even if the great majority of schools may presently be structured to do just the opposite (1).

Based on the above, it appears that the real key to the educability concept is self-direction in learning. Dave (1975) recognized this by suggesting that educability, while a broader concept, "...is a concomitant outcome of (self-directed learning) since the educability of an individual is enhanced further as self-managed learning is increasingly carried out" (p.50). In order to address educability, evaluation must be able to recognize self-direction in learners as well as assess characteristics of learners that lead to self-direction. It must also be ready to assess aspects of the learning environment that might contribute to the development of self-direction.

RECOGNIZING SELF-DIRECTION IN LEARNING. Self-direction in learning should not be difficult to identify in the behavior of individuals and groups. It is intentional, involving choice on the learner's part rather than imposition by an external agent; it is characterized by competence in planning and execution; and it reveals persistence in the attainment of objectives.

Tough's (1971) studies of adult learning defined self-directed learning (though he did not use the term) biographically. "Deliberate adult learning" occurs when individuals engage in a series of connected "learning episodes" together forming a "learning project." The criteria for a learning episode in Tough's studies appear to be straightforward. A given activity constituted a learning episode if it had the following characteristics:

1. The learning that occurs is *intentional* (as compared to accidental or incidental). This intent remains dominant throughout the learning episode.

2. The learner engages in the activity in order to develop some reasonably *definite knowledge or skill* rather than for general self-improvement without a prior decision as to what the nature of that self-improvement might be. Tough defines "knowledge and skill" very broadly, including any kind of intentional change in the learner from the relatively trivial to the fundamental, and including harmful as well as useful changes.

3. The learner wishes to *retain* the knowledge or skills for some definite period of time. In Tough's studies the period of intended retention required for classifying a given activity as a learning episode varied from a few days to a lifetime.

4. The intention to learn some definite knowledge or skill must be the *predominant motive* for engaging in the activity. In Tough's terminology "predominant" means "more than half of the person's motivations" (2).

While others might choose somewhat different criteria, Tough's work does support the assertion that self-direction in learning can be recognized relatively easily. Self-directed learners can be recognized because they choose to engage in intentional learning activities for the purpose of developing and retaining some definite knowledge or skill. Unfortunately, it is by no means as easy to identify the kinds of personal characteristics (constructs) self-directed learners possess nor to describe with confidence the nature of learning settings that promote the development of self-direction in learners.

Personal Characteristics of Self-Directed Learners

In developing hypotheses about personal characteristics that lead to self-direction in learning, it is necessary to move from the overtly behavioral to the theoretical, to ask what people who engage in self-directed learning might be like. This kind of thinking is essential for reasons advanced in the self-awareness example. It helps to build theories about educational practice. It also orients evaluation to consider what kinds of constructs should be assessed, both in the learner and in the context in which learning occurs.

Basic social science research and theory has long anticipated the current interest in the self-direction aspects of the educability concept. Berlyne's (1965) chapter "Curiosity and Education" ties together a variety of strands of work in comparative and social psychology on conditions leading to behavior that is intrinsically, rather than extrinsically, motivated. Conditions of novelty, incongruity, and complexity have been observed to elicit exploratory behavior in both humans and animals. "Epistemic" behavior, or behavior which builds up knowledge, is facilitated by what Berlyne referred to as "discovery" methods in the learning situation.

Philosophical concepts such as Maslow's (1954) *self-actualization* or Roger's (1969) *experiential learning* are grounded on the idea of continuous self-development that is intrinsically initiated and maintained. A number of the criteria for lifelong education listed in the first chapter under Self-Growth, Self-Directed Learning, and Democratization reflect this same kind of emphasis. At the societal level, these kinds of characteristics in individuals plus an atmosphere conducive to "interlearning" would lead in Dave's (1975) analysis to what has come to be known as a "learning society."

Self-direction in learning is clearly dependent on Dave's (1973) first four clusters of skills and competencies. Without requisite cognitive and other skills, self-direction in learning would amount to self-misdirection! Most of the other writers who have dealt with educability also propose constructs that deal with skills and competencies as well as constructs

that reflect aspects of self-direction (3). The concern here
is only with the latter. The list that follows is synthesized
from a number of sources, especially Berlyne (1965), Biggs
(1973), Dave (1975), March (1972), Maslow (1954), Joyce and
Weil (1972), Rogers (1969) and Wroczyñski (1974), as well as
from the evaluative criteria summarized in the report by Skager
and Dave (1977) (4). The list is doubtless incomplete and can
do no more than anticipate the next stage of work on the concept of educability. In addition, the various constructs are
likely to be interpreted somewhat differently - and differentially valued - in various societal contexts. All would probably be perceived as desirable in societies that value a high
degree of individualism, but some might be perceived as less
desirable in societies that stress a high level of co-operative-
ness.

SELF-ACCEPTANCE. This construct has already been illustrated in some detail. As used here, self-acceptance refers to positive views about the self as a
learner. It is grounded in extensive and successful
prior experience. Biggs (1973) uses "appropriate self-
concept" to refer to a similar construct. However,
not only does self-acceptance mean "I can do it", as
Biggs suggests, it also refers to a positive valuing
of the self as an entity worthy of improvement.

PLANFULNESS. Planful learners are able to (a) diagnose their own learning needs, (b) set appropriate
personal goals in the light of those needs, and (c)
devise effective strategies for accomplishing the
learning goals. Such individuals may utilize the
help and advice of others at any stage in the above
process, but it is because they choose to do so. The
planful learner may also arrive at such personal goals
during the learning process, e.g., may engage in learning for the purpose of goal setting.

INTRINSIC MOTIVATION. Learners who are intrinsically motivated persist in learning activity in the
absence of external controls in the form of rewards
or sanctions. They are likely to continue learning
outside of formal learning situations and to delay
or even forego various kinds of competing gratifica-
tions in order to proceed with learning.

INTERNALIZED EVALUATION. Self-directed learners are

able to act as their own evaluation agents. They can
give accurate estimates of the quality of their own
performance based on evidence they collect themselves.
Learners who have internalized the evaluation process
may solicit feedback on their own performance from
knowledgeable others, but they will accept external
evaluation as valid only when the qualifications of
the judge are established independently of social
role and when the evaluation agrees with their own
evidence.

OPENNESS TO EXPERIENCE. Learners who are open to experience engage in new kinds of activities that may
result in learning or goal setting. However, conscious-
ness that either of the latter may occur is not necessarily the reason for entering into new kinds of activity. Curiosity, tolerance for ambiguity, preference
for complexity, and even playfulness (all cited by
other authors) represent motives for entering into
new activities and imply openness to experience. Further delineation of this construct may reveal that it
comprises several component constructs.

FLEXIBILITY. Flexibility in learning implies a willingness to change goals or learning mode and to use
exploratory, trial and error approaches to problems.
It does not imply a lack or persistence in learning
itself. Failure is countered with adaptive behavior
rather than by withdrawal.

AUTONOMY. Autonomous learners choose to engage in
types of learning that may not be seen as important
(or that may even be perceived as dangerous) within
a particular cultural context. Such individuals are
able to question the normative standards of a given
time and place as to what kinds of learning are valuable and permissible. However, such autonomy is exercised by the learner in the service of a wider per-
ception of personal and social utility.

The proposed list of constructs relating to self-direction
in learning presents a most formidable set of open educational
goals. To what extent education alone, especially school education, affects the development of such traits in individuals is
certainly a matter for debate. Developing means of assessing
these goals as manifested in the behavior of learners and relat-

ing such assessments to the conditions under which learning
takes place is a major task for evaluation under lifelong education. Many writers already assign a major role to the school
of these areas. The radical educational reformers discussed
by Hargreaves (1974), in spite of sharp disagreement as to
whether society needs schools at all, would almost surely agree
to the proposition that schools play a major role in the genesis
of such characteristics. The traditional, rigidly organized,
inflexible, and elitist school is seen by both pro and anti-
school reformers as having a massively suppressive effect on
the development of self-direction in learners. This same assumption is abundantly evident in the literature on lifelong education. That the school as an institution has a critical influence on self-direction is perhaps the most fundamental tenet
of modern reformist thought in education.

Educating for Self-Direction in Learners

There is hardly a lack of ideas as to how learners can be
helped to be more independent in all aspects of their approach
to learning. All of these ideas involve the creation of learning contexts in which individuals are free to exercise various
types of independence. Some proposed contexts even make it impossible for the learner to progress at all without exercising
self-direction. Suchman's (1966) "inquiry training" model in
which learners must generate principles that explain events is
an example of the latter.

Locus of control of the learning function is thus the basic
concern for contemporary theories about the development of self-
direction. There are obviously levels of control in the learning process which might form a scale of hierarchy. At each of
the levels a variety of implementation techniques can be conceived. For example, Flechsig sees control in the learning
situation as proceeding through four stages (5).

1. The context in which the learner is located controls all aspects of the learning process.

2. The place at which learning takes place is under
   the control of the learner.

3. Choice of the mode of learning is under the control of the learner.

4. Choice of the ecology is left to the learner,

e.g., the learner is free to select any kind of
delivery system including completely independent
learning.

Flechsig's analysis does suggest critical points at which
self-direction in learning might be facilitated. However, it
leaves out the inevitably controversial issue of whether or not
the learner should choose the *content* of learning. Certainly
in most societies there are many situations in which it is acceptable for learners to select their own content. Deliberate
learning for self-improvement that is not related to any desire
to advance the self in a work or social role is the most obvious example. But societies support formal education for definite communal ends that have nothing to do with the needs or
proclivities of individuals. Illiteracy among members of an
advanced technological society is not only wrong from a human-
itarian point of view, it is damaging to the society as a whole.
Illiterates are less likely to be able to make intelligent
choices in politics, work, and personal life. They are less
likely to be productive and more likely to require support from
other members of the society. Likewise, it makes no sense for
a society to have ten times as many architects or lawyers as
it needs, while at the same time facing serious shortages of
qualified engineers and technicians. Yet many societies, especially in the less developed world, face this type of problem.

Total control by learners themselves over selection of the
content of learning thus has important social implications. It
would probably be viewed with intense skepticism in virtually
all societies, especially in reference to learning at the level
of the school. Yet writers such as Postman and Weingartner
(1969) appear to propose exactly this. Even compulsory school
attendance has been questioned in the writings of Holt (1972).
At the level of higher education Cross (1975) has proposed a
"pluralistic model" which eschews the requirement that individuals meet any common criteria for admittance to universities,
or that they emerge with at least some common skills, competencies, or knowledgeabilities.

Positions like the above have probably gone far beyond the
practical need to find ways to encourage self-direction in learning. They quite obviously devolve from an ideology and reflect
consistency with an all-embracing principle. Yet, choice of
content does occur even in traditional educational settings.
Learners typically proceed through stages in which more and
more freedom is allowed in the selection of educational content.

Younger children select books and projects. Older children often choose electives around a core curriculum. Young adults choose whether to engage in various kinds of training oriented toward a particular vocation or whether to enter higher education. They choose fields of study and specializations within those fields. None of this means that the learner's role as a selector of educational content does not deserve a great deal of further exploration. But it does suggest that there are limits, that modern societies cannot afford to have substantial proportions of their citizens either under-educated or irrelevantly educated. It also implies a maturational approach to choice behavior. It assumes that, as individuals mature in an appropriate environment, they are increasingly able to choose intelligently as well as to make more important kinds of choices. The real question concerns the kinds of environments that are appropriate.

THE ROLE OF EDUCATIONAL MODELS. Models are systems of interrelated concepts or constructs. Used descriptively, models focus on the essential characteristics of a given phenomenon from a particular perspective. Descriptions of the events occurring in a classroom could vary considerably if the observations were made from the perspective of markedly different educational models, since events that are important in one model might be ignored in another. Models are also used in the design of educational practice. They define at a conceptual level what the learning context is to be like.

A number of models emphasizing self-direction in learning have already been proposed. Many more will doubtless be invented. The purpose here is not to present the models themselves but rather to suggest a set of descriptive dimensions by which the members of this particular family of models can be described and compared. These dimensions appear to represent aspects of the learning situation that are most likely to facilitate self-directed learning. Designers of different learning models will implement the dimensions in different ways. But collectively, it appears likely that models of self-directed learning will stress aspects of the learning situation listed below.

Conditions that Lead to Self-Directed Learning

The following dimensions of the learning situation each embody one or more educational principles. An effort has been made to state them in a way which involves a minimum amount of overlap. The dimensions define continua that could be used to generate evaluative profiles of various learning contexts. Different models of educating for self-direction would have different profiles, depending on the particular dimensions stressed. There are inevitably some interrelationships among the dimensions in that the intensity of one dimension may affect the intensity of another. Still, the dimensions do represent sufficiently distinct aspects of the learning situation to be useful for constructing profiles.

FLEXIBILITY IN TIME, PLACE, MODE, AND CONTENT OF LEARNING. Flexibility is a basic principle of lifelong education. Without flexibility of time, place, mode, and content, learners would never have the chance to exercise choice, would not have opportunities to become adept at a variety of modes of learning, and would be unable to follow their own interests and proclivities, perhaps never learning to trust their own intrinsic motives for certain types of learning. Flexibility is a condition that is antecedent to the operation of other conditions relating to self-directed learning. As conceived here, it actually incorporates four-component dimensions (time, place, mode, and content) that are reasonably independent of one another and that could readily be assessed formally or informally. Flexibility alone does not necessarily mean complete freedom of choice, or even that the learner does any of the choosing.

MAXIMIZING APPROPRIATE OPPORTUNITIES FOR CHOICE ON THE PART OF LEARNERS. The potential importance of giving learners opportunities for choosing was apparent in the hierarchy of self-direction proposed by Flechsig. It is commonly assumed that learners must be given experience with choosing if they are to learn to choose willingly and effectively. In addition to time, place, mode, and content, learners may also choose or set their own evaluative criteria - how well they want to perform. The qualification implied in the idea of "appropriate" opportunity for choice means that the maturity of the learner and the practical needs of the society must be taken into account, especially it seems in the area of choice of educational content.

EMPHASIS ON FACILITATING ASPECTS OF TEACHING. The role of the teacher is naturally a matter of intense concern in thinking about self-direction in learning. Tough (1971) gives the reminder that the teacher's role as evaluator is frequently in conflict with the teacher's role as helper. When learners unquestioningly accept direction by the teacher because they fear a negative evaluation if they do not, ingrained dependency may

be the result. Yet it would be absurd to suggest that persons
in the role of teacher can avoid exercising the evaluative function. Failure to provide learners with feedback on the quality
of their performance is to deprive them of meaning. Even recognition on the part of the teacher that the learner needs help
is bound to be perceived by the latter as stemming from an evaluation. Rather, the need is for an appropriate emphasis, (that
is to say one suited to the learner's level of e.g. maturity)
to be placed on the helping or facilitating role of the teacher
in contrast to his role as judge or evaluator. Tough (1971)
summarizes a number of personal characteristics of effective
helpers in the learning situation (see his Appendix C).

ENCOURAGING LEARNERS TO BECOME THEIR OWN EVALUATIVE AGENTS.
How learners may be encouraged to assume the role of internal
evaluation agent is perhaps the number one question in conceptualizing curricula supportive of self-directed learning. There
is no evidence for the radical proposition that simply removing
external evaluation will have the effect of fostering self-direction. However, research by Maher and Stallings (1972) does
suggest that learners characterized by high need to achieve are
more likely to select and persist in complex learning tasks
under conditions of intrinsic motivation and less willing to
work on easy tasks, the latter being more preferred when evaluation is external. Rogers (1969) suggests that learners first
have to learn to generate their own evaluative criteria. This
can be done under the so-called "contract system" in which
learners set their own performance goals and work until those
goals have been achieved, with the value to be placed on achievement of the goal determined in advance.

Perhaps the most interesting general principle for promoting self-evaluation is expressed in Moore's (1963) notion of
the "responsive environment." Associated with simulation and
cybernetic learning theory, the responsive environment is arranged so as to provide immediate feedback to the learner without reliance on external human evaluation agents.

Joyce and Weil (1972) suggest that responsive environments
provide learners with direct feedback on the quality of their
performance without at the same time furnishing the correct
answer or action. However, less elaborate means of delivering
the curriculum than those proposed by Moore contain elements
of responsiveness. It is certainly a feature of self-instructional materials which incorporate built-in evaluation devices
administered by the learner. The principle is to provide the

learner with direct and immediate feedback, while at the same
time minimizing the need to depend on other individuals, especially individuals in positions of authority. There are obviously many ways of applying this principle, and it may be a
very powerful agent in helping learners internalize the evaluation function.

ENCOURAGING DEMOCRATIC RELATIONSHIPS IN THE LEARNING SITUA-
TION. There is an obvious incompatibility between the authority
dominated learning situation and the development of independence
on the part of learners. The need for more democratic relationships between teachers and students and between students themselves is also so generally recognized in the literature on lifelong education that this principle, like locus of control, cannot be associated with a few individuals. This need is obviously related to locus of control, but deals with the structure of
social relationships rather than with whether or not learners
are encouraged to make certain kinds of choices. It does not
disallow authority, but would base authority on competence
rather than on irrelevant status criteria. It emphasizes what
Spady (1977) refers to as "collaborative" decision making and
generally reflects the democratization theme of lifelong education. The reformist conception of the teaching role in Harg-
reave's (1974) analysis is perhaps the most fully articulated
view of this altered pattern of relationships between teacher
and learner.

CAPITALIZING ON THE INTRINSIC MOTIVES OF THE LEARNER.
Berlyne's (1965) discussion of epistemic curiosity as a motivating force in learning has already been referred to. Discovery
methods elicit intentional learning behavior by inducing conceptual conflict in the learner leading to efforts to resolve
the conflict. Situations which induce such conflict according
to Berlyne are designed so as to induce (a) surprise, (b) doubt,
(c) perplexity, (d) bafflement, or (e) contradiction in the
learner's mind. Moore's (1963) concept of "autotelic" activity,
or learning engaged in for its own sake, is closely related.
Discovery learning, however, is modeled more on the formal process of scientific discovery. Moore's analysis is modeled
primarily on puzzles and games of strategy or chance, as well
as on symbolic play.

Learning through games and puzzles is a long-used educational tool. If situations are designed cleverly enough, abstract material such as arithmetic may be learned in concrete
situations in which applications of the abstractions are im-

mediately apparent to the learner. This tactic is also useful
in language learning as well as in many other areas of educational content.

EMPHASIS ON EXPRESSIVE EDUCATIONAL OBJECTIVES. Eisner's
(1968) expressive objectives confront learners with problems to
be solved, as noted early in this chapter. These are open-ended
problems in which the path to solution as well as the form of
the solution is under the control of the learner. Solution of
such problems by definition depends on the exercise of self-
direction. Biggs (1973) suggests that problems should be structured so that "initially vague intentions become precise as
performance progresses." Wroczynski (1974) apparently proposes
a similar emphasis in his concept of "problem-centered" instruction, although the teacher probably exercises more control of
the problem-solving process in this conception than in that
proposed by Biggs. However, Wroczyñski does assign the learner
a primary role in formulating the problem.

ORIENTING LEARNING TO PERFORMANCE IN LIFE ROLES BY INCOR-
PORATING LEARNING OUTSIDE THE SCHOOL. Spady (1977) stresses
the importance of expanding the concept of instruction to include outside resource specialists not on the regular school
staff and of locating a significant proportion of learning in
the larger community. This is yet another articulation of the
principle of Horizontal Integration. However, the deliberate
relating of learning and life role may have special significance
in the encouragement of self-direction. It therefore seems
reasonable that learners be oriented as early as possible to
the need for learning in life situations and to the fact that
learning need not be confined behind the walls of the school.

Relationships between Conditions and Learner Characteristics

The eight conditions for facilitating self-direction in
learners have been selected because they represent plausible
hypotheses about how the earlier set of learner characteristics
might be developed. There is not necessarily a one-to-one relationship between learning conditions and learner characteristics.
In the former case, emphasis is on principles that have potentially broad and interactive effects. Still, some correspondence is evident, as for example between internalized evaluation in the learner and the principle of encouraging learners
to become their own evaluation agents, or between intrinsic
motivation in the learner and the corresponding instructional
principle.

The eight characteristics of the learning environment just proposed are hypotheses that should in the long run be testable, though certainly only in evaluative research that would extend over relatively long periods of time and that would place heavy emphasis on the collection of biographical data on the individuals. Indeed, such work would amount to systematic educational biography. As admitted earlier, it is not really known what evaluations of the impact of the school will reveal, in spite of the assumptions of many educational reformers. But the two lists of personal and situational characteristics do provide constructs around which evaluation instruments and procedures can be built. They suggest what to look for in the learner as well as in the learning situation.

Conclusion

The general concept of open educational goals incorporates the more specific concept (though it is still inclusive enough) of self-directed learning. Lifelong education now badly needs to define its concepts, especially those that suggest goals of the open variety. The first half of the chapter for that reason dealt with the definition of personal and situational constructs and provided one example of the use of personal constructs in the process of building links between educational goals and actual educational practices. Personal constructs, in turn, serve as starting points in the development of evaluative measures.

Open educational goals have been most fully articulated in the unifying concept of educability. With respect to the latter, self-direction in learning seems to be the key component concept. At the level of the individual and the instructional process the facilitation of self-direction is absolutely vital to the implementation of lifelong education. It is hoped that the synthesis of the literature which was attempted in the second half of the chapter will have clarified the kinds of learner characteristics which may be hypothesized to promote self-direction as well as the nature of learning situations that may aid in its development.

NOTES

1. Hargreaves (1974) in his concepts of "Deschoolers" and "New Romantics" presents an excellent comparative analysis of these two incompatible viewpoints.

2. Tough's attempt to estimate the predominant motivational source underlying an individual's learning activities might seem to pose insurmountable measurement problems. However, it is actually possible to make such estimates in a reasonably objective way given that the learner has no reason for hiding his real motives. For example, Tough and his associates had individuals distribute 100 points between various reasons for engaging in a learning activity. If more than 50 points were assigned to motives such as pleasure, relaxation, or interest in content unaccompanied by a desire for retention, the activity was not classified as a learning episode. If more than 50 points were assigned to motives such as the desire to develop a particular skill or to retain some kind of content, then the activity was so classified.

3. Related terms often used in discussions of self-direction in learning are "autonomy" and "auto-didactics" (Frederiksson & Gestrelius, 1975). These terms have not been used here because they have the connotation of working alone. Self-directed learners might well turn to others for help and feedback or choose to work in a learning group. A self-directed learner could choose any means of learning and depend extensively on the help and co-operation of other learners or teachers and still be self-directed in the sense of setting personal goals, internalizing the evaluation process, etc.

4. I am also indebted to the consultants listed in the Foreword for a number of useful suggestions.

5. Personal communication from Professor Karl-Heinz Flechsig of the University of Göttingen.

CHAPTER 5

FUTURE LINES OF DEVELOPMENT FOR EVALUATION UNDER LIFELONG EDUCATION

This book has explored the probable nature of evaluation under lifelong education. The task has admittedly been undertaken in the face of at least one significant handicap: lifelong education as fully developed strategy for organizing education within a society does not yet exist anywhere. It remains a set of relatively abstract principles.

Evaluation needs a concrete subject matter. In itself it does not create curricula, models of teaching, or systems for delivering educational content to potential consumers. In this sense, this report might seem to be premature. It is an attempt to describe the needs of an evaluation practice that would be appropriate to a concept of education that has so far not been implemented. This is important. Evaluation is a disruptive activity if its form does not fit the phenomena it addresses. Biggs (1973) certainly had this in mind in suggesting that (for L-Evaluation "...instructional and evaluational procedures typically lead to incompatible messages."

Fortunately, while lifelong education as a total, organizing system does not exist anywhere, its component elements have been evident for some time in various forms and degrees. There is little that is new about lifelong education other than the fact that it is a comprehensive scheme for organizing an entire society educationally. But virtually all of its principles have been and are being tried out on a small scale, or, for societies as a whole, to a limited degree. The Faure, et al. (1972) report is built around specific examples already operating in various countries, so that a visible subject matter is not entirely lacking.

In the last two chapters, evaluation criteria for lifelong education were examined in terms of the distinction between specified and open educational goals. Here the main objective was to determine what kinds of information would be most relevant for evaluation within an educational system organized according to the principles of lifelong education. The vital functions of crediting and certifying human accomplishment were shown to underscore the need for accurate and fair means of assessing the attainment of specified educational goals. This assessment need inevitably leads to a consideration of new techniques for specifying content domains and interpreting performance within those domains in terms of content mastery.

Likewise, lifelong education's central concern with the enhancement of educability and especially the cluster of open goals relating to self-direction in learning introduces a mainly new subject matter for evaluation. This subject matter can be assessed at present only in a rudimentary fashion. Constructs referring to the personal characteristics of self-directed learners and to the dimensions of learning situations that enhance self-direction need to be stated as precisely as possible. Without precision in this area, it will be impossible to build evaluation instruments and procedures that have any chance of being valid measures of the phenomena they are meant to address.

The form of evaluation under lifelong education has been mainly ignored since the second chapter. In evaluation, as in biology, form follows function, but is in this case also likely to be affected by the nature of the evaluation agent. Given the consensus among authorities on lifelong education that the negative aspects of contemporary evaluation practice, particularly those aspects of L-Evaluation having a strong impact on the learner in L-Evaluation, are to be avoided, as well as the earlier predicted emphasis on internal evaluation agents and formative evaluative functions, it is possible to anticipate that less formal approaches to evaluation will be taken much more seriously under lifelong education than they are at present. Just what those "less formal" approaches may be and why they should be explored in future work merits mention in this concluding chapter.

Three areas of future inquiry relating to the development of evaluation practice have been identified for this purpose. The first two devolve from the fundamental distinction made in this report between specified and open goals and the third to the form that evaluation practice is likely to take under lifelong education. This report will conclude with brief discussions of the kinds of work that now appear to be needed in each of these three areas.

I. Developing Crediting and Certifying Systems Compatible with Formal, Informal and Non-formal Types of Lifelong Education

It has been emphasized throughout this report that the ascendence of lifelong education at the societal level rests entirely on the assumption that learning acquired by non-formal and informal means will have the same status as learning acquired in the formal institutions of school and university. The role that certifying and crediting systems must play in this process seems self-evident. It is not only essential that such systems be developed, but also that they are legitimized through rigorous formulation and through acceptance by the general public as well as by those who allocate educational resources and opportunities.

General acceptance of evaluation systems that assess what individuals do in terms of specified learning goals and objectives implies a dramatic shift from the contemporary situation in which it is really educational institutions that are certified (accredited) rather than learners. If learners have engaged in whatever processes the institution has to offer over an approved span of time, and have managed to compete successfully with other learners during that period, then a formal school degree is granted as a symbol of credit. Educational institutions in most societies still advance students on the basis of their relative standing among a reference group of peers. This kind of evaluation system relies wholly on the legitimacy of a formal institution as the primary vehicle for bringing about socially useful kinds of learning. But the crediting or certification which such institutions provide rarely, if ever, tells us exactly what the learner *knows* or can *do*. The traditional L-Evaluation system is thus useless as a guide for recognizing and crediting skills and accomplishments in individuals who have utilized modes of education other than schooling.

The alternative to crediting and certifying on the basis of institutional legitimacy has never been attempted on any large scale. Its implementation demands careful specification of content and performance domains in education and work. The third chapter surveyed on-going work on the development of a measurement technology relevant to this end. But at the soci-

etal level mere technology is insufficient. What is needed is
a conception of how such a system would operate if the technology is to be put to use. In thinking along these lines, it is
necessary to recognize that a comprehensive system for crediting educational accomplishment and certifying work capability
would amount to a very powerful new institution within a society. Its development, locus of authority, and relationships
with other institutions would introduce significant political
considerations relating to how the system is to be shaped and
controlled. Members of existing institutions, above all those
identified with formal schooling, would undoubtedly make a
strong case for their right of control. Those who would seek
to represent informal and non-formal educational modes would
make their own case. Representatives of industry and agricul-
ture could also claim the right to control, especially for the
certification function.

There is thus a prospect of considerable competition among
different institutional components of a society over the nature
and control of any comprehensive system for crediting and certifying educational attainment. It is easy to speculate that
the dominance of any one faction could have a decisive effect
on the continued viability of another, particularly within the
educational sphere itself. If representatives of formal schooling were to dominate, it is likely that attainment by formal
and informal means would remain an inferior mode of accomplishment. If those not identified with formal schooling were to
gain the upper hand, then schools themselves could be seriously
weakened as institutions. Deprived of responsibility for summative evaluation in the form of degrees or certificates, they
might lose effective control over the curriculum and would
perhaps perceive a considerably lessened need to maintain standards. This, indeed, would be one mechanism for "de-schooling"
society.

It is therefore abundantly clear that imaginative (and
careful) conceptual work is needed toward the goal of defining
alternative models for implementing crediting and certifying
systems on a national scale. It is most unlikely that a single
model would be viable across societies that are at different
stages of development or that are organized under different
political systems. But all models would have to take into account how different interests within a society can make constructive contributions both to (a) the control and management
of the system and (b) the specification of what kinds of knowledge and skills are relevant to each of the many content do-

mains that would ultimately be assessed.

In all models the role of government would be a key variable. A crediting and certifying system could be envisaged as a government agency under a charter of authority independent of the various social institutions that would serve as the vehicles for delivering educational opportunity to the public. Alternatively, the system could be sanctioned and coordinated through government's educational authority but run through a non-governmental agency formed through the collaboration of institutions which might otherwise be in competition for the allocation of educational resources. Clearly, a number of models can and should be developed for the operation of crediting and certifying at the societal level.

Meanwhile, work on the technology of domain specification and assessment for mastery will go on. It should have been apparent from the discussion in Chapter 3 that much of this work is already far enough advanced to be applied on a larger scale than is presently the case. The development of model systems for applying this technology as well as its formal tryout in various situations, especially where attainment was through non-formal and informal means, should serve to stimulate further developments. It thus appears to be an appropriate time to take a detailed *technical* look at present and anticipated capabilities in the assessment of specified goals. Optimal strategies for utilizing what is known can be derived from such a technical analysis, and these strategies would in turn complement the development of model certification and crediting systems.

The technical analysis should first incorporate a careful evaluation of available methods for generating content for specified goal domains. Distinctions should be made between the various approaches to defining precise content domains designed primarily for the crediting of *educational* accomplishment as compared to methods such as criterion sampling that are more adapted to certifying performance in *work*. It is quite likely that empirical studies would devolve from such a comparative analysis. The nature of a mastery interpretation for each generation mode would also have to be examined.

A second facet of the technical analysis would be concerned with measures of the quality of domain-referenced assessment devices. Especially important would be the reliability of such measures in various contexts and for various types of decisions.

The appropriateness of various test or other assessment formats for different cultures would also be an important consideration.

A third type of work would immediately follow the model-building and technical analysis. Its success would depend on the prior existence of small scale crediting and certification systems, preferably in countries with differing social systems or at different levels of development. This empirical work would focus on factors that relate to the successful implementation of crediting and certifying systems in different social environments, including factors of cost in time and resources as well as structural and attitudinal barriers within each social system. The perceived legitimacy of non-school-based learner evaluation systems would certainly be an important component of the latter, especially among those who have greatest influence on resource allocation for education.

The case study would probably constitute an especially appropriate methodology for examining the implementation of prototype crediting and certifying systems. Case study methods require extensive involvement on the part of the researcher with the phenomena under study. This involvement is accompanied by informed analysis, classification, and organization of the observations. The latter should in turn result in a theory or conceptualization about the implementation of crediting and certifying systems on a large scale basis, related, it may be hoped, to the characteristics of different societies.

The three types of research and development activities proposed above should contribute significantly to the process of evaluation for specified goals under lifelong education. Indeed, without such work it is difficult to imagine how the principles of lifelong education could be successfully implemented in any modern society, since there would be no reliable and fair means to credit educational accomplishment irrespective of the manner in which it was attained.

II. Development of Criteria and Strategies for Assessing Self-Direction in Learning and Facilitating Self-Direction in the Learning Context

Open-ended goals relating to self-direction in learning were identified in the fourth chapter as the key element of the educability concept. These goals were seen as both personal (characteristic of learners) and situational (characteristics of the context in which learning takes place). In this discussion, it was suggested that, while self-direction can be recognized in learner behavior, the relevant personal characteristics of learners who engage in such behavior remain to be identified. What is it that schools and other forms of education should attempt to foster in learners, both as individuals and as cooperating members of learning communities? It is equally important that dimensions of the learning environment likely to facilitate the development and expression of such characteristics be identified. A start was made on both of these tasks through a preliminary synthesis of pertinent literature. This work has only begun, however.

The personal and situational constructs hypothesized to relate to self-direction in learning need to be examined in the light of a complete review of available conceptualizations and research findings. This is no small task. It is equally important that before they are defined further the constructs proposed in the previous chapter be reviewed from the perspective of different social and political systems. Lifelong education is an internationally promulgated conception of education. Its concepts need to be defined in a way that promotes maximum generality of application. Any individual educational writer works within the perspective of his or her own cultural experience. It is vital that any conclusions be tested within different cultural perspectives. The culmination of this process would be a full and generalizable elaboration of relevant personal and situational constructs for the purposes of (a) constructing educational theories about how self-direction may be facilitated and (b) constructing assessment instruments for use in evaluation. The latter would include instruments and procedures for assessing the characteristics of learners as well as the nature of the situation in which learning takes place.

The next stage of work, perhaps not very far removed in time if early work proceeds quickly enough, involves the study of learners in contexts designed to promote self-direction. The goals of such research must be modest in the short-run. Links between educational contexts, personal characteristics of learners, and self-directed learning behavior will be very complex, if indeed there are causal links at all, especially for the first two classes of phenomena. As suggested earlier, only an approach incorporating long-term educational biography is likely to give genuinely meaningful information about self-directed learning as a stable characteristic of learners. Even here the picture would inevitably be significantly influenced by the supportiveness of the larger social context.

In the shorter run it is possible to pursue two lines of work. First, evaluation instruments and procedures for assessing personal and situational constructs relating to self-direction should be developed and tested for applicability to various learning and societal contexts. In such research, it would also be important to determine whether the L-Evaluation instruments actually differentiate between learners who behave in a self-directed manner and those who generally do not, as well as whether the C-Evaluation procedures differentiate between educational contexts designed to promote self-direction and those of a more traditional type. This type of work would allow for at least a preliminary evaluation of the generalizability and validity of assessment procedures.

Finally, experience gained through try-outs of evaluation procedures can be applied to the revision of the constructs from which they were derived. If comparative international research of this type were undertaken, the results would be a set of revised constructs which would have considerable generality of application and unusual comparability across different societies. Later research undertaken in different national and cultural contexts would as a result be more likely to contribute to a common body of knowledge. All of this would hopefully lead to a better understanding of the personal characteristics of self-directed learners and the possible influence of schools and other educational contexts on the development of those characteristics.

III. Appraising the Value of Non-Formal or Qualitative Research Strategies and the Method of Advocacy

This report has been written from a mainly formal perspective on the nature of the information gathering process in evaluation. It is true that nothing has been said about the necessity of forming control groups through the random assignment of learners to treatment conditions, about the importance of unequivocal research designs, nor about the value of statistical tests of significance. This "neo-positivistic" laboratory research model admittedly dominates evaluation as it is currently practised and written about in many parts of the world. It should indeed be obvious that this tradition has been the dominant one influencing this book. But the tradition itself has not been dealt with in these pages because it has been written about extensively already, both pro and con, and there appears to be little to add to the discussion. Suffice it to say that the formal research paradigm as far as evaluation is concerned should be viewed as *a* strategy of inquiry, but not as *the* strategy of inquiry.

The bias (if that is what it is) towards the formal has been reflected here in an emphasis on issues relating to measurement. The discussion of chapters 3 and 4 on specified and open educational goals have assumed that evaluative data are quantitative and that relevant events can be expressed as symbols with one or more properties of the number system. It now needs to be said that there are alternatives to quantification as well as to the laboratory research model, and that these alternatives deserve exploration. This is especially the case within the perspective of lifelong education. The relevance of internal evaluation agents and formative evaluation noted in the first chapter argues for the more frequent use of qualitative information and non-formal approaches to obtaining that information.

In the days when artisans learned their professions through apprenticeship to a master craftsman with whom they had constant contact over a long period of time, there was no need for a measurement technology incorporating content referenced instruments and mastery interpretations based on statistical probability theory. Evidence of the learner's level of competency was direct and available. Certification was the prerogative of the master and the instrument his experience and judgment. Romantic as this older way of doing things may seem, it is mainly incompatible with the nature of modern technological societies. Still, the fact that information is non-quantitative does not mean that it is by definition invalid, nor is information of lesser importance because it was not collected in a controlled experiment.

The gap between research and practice in education, as in other fields of applied social science, has stimulated inquiry into the process of change itself, as in the work of Havelock (1971) and Huberman (1973) cited in the initial chapter. The distinction made there between the research and development and the human relations/problem-solving models of the change process is very close to the distinction which can be made between two sharply contrasting approaches to social science research itself: *the positivistic* research approach of the laboratory experiment whose defining characteristic is a separation between the researcher and the phenomenon being researched versus *action research* in which the researcher is a knowing and known participant in the process under investigation. In the first model, the guiding principle is objectivity, in the second, it is bringing about change. Much more is known about the former in connection with evaluation, but relatively little about the latter.

Identified with the psychologist Kurt Lewin, action research almost seems to have been deliberately designed as an approach to conducting formative C-Evaluation. It is interventionistic and utilizes what have here been referred to as internal agents. Four subtypes of action research are identified by Chein, Cook, and Harding (1948). These writers see community interest rather than scientific discipline as determining the choice of problem for the action researcher. But application of findings is the primary goal of the action researcher. "Not only must he make discoveries, but he must see to it that his discoveries are applied" (Chein, et al., 1948).

The potential of action research as an evaluation strategy needs to be explored, and at least one such exploration is currently underway under the direction of Professor Christoph Wulf. Action research clearly is a potential alternative to positivistic inquiry. While apparently antithetical, the two approaches could coexist. As alternatives, they could be used to confirm or invalidate one another.

Irrespective of whether one or the other research strategy is selected, there still remains the question of the use of qualitative information in evaluation. Such information is used even at present in the form of anecdotal reports, descriptive material, and the like. But in most cases, it does not have the status that is usually assigned to quantitative information in the form of tables, graphs, and statistics. Moreover, qualitative information is derived from methods of inquiry that are seen as "softer" (less rigorous) than research within the experimental paradigm. Yet these methods generate types of information that experimental research methods rarely, if ever, achieve. Participants in the educational process acting as internal evaluation agents are also likely to see qualitative methods as more relevant.

The *case study* has already been mentioned. This method requires close familiarity with the situation under examination. Here the observer is by no means an ordinary participant, but rather an especially knowledgeable person who is likely to bring experience and judgment to the study that is not available to the typical participant. Bennis (1968) makes this point clear by tracing the origins of the case study to the Hippocratic method in medicine. Indeed, the physician is the natural role model for the social scientist or other professional conducting a case study. Physicians are in the situation, but as informed observers. Patients do not write their own case studies.

Many experimentalists would doubtless maintain that the case study not only produces qualitative rather than quantitative information, but is also not generalizable beyond the situation in question. This type of criticism is a two-edged sword, since most evaluations using an experimental approach are also conducted in special situations where it is impossible to apply principles such as randomization to the selection of units of observations or to maintain rigorous control over competing influences that may affect both internal and external validity. To believe that generalizable knowledge can be garnered only through the experimental research strategem is to deny the validity of most modes of human experience as systematized in various social science research methods. As Levine (1974) suggests, this restricted point of view is not good science, it is idolatry. The utility of the case study for evaluation deserves full exploration, and Stodolsky (1975) has already made a case for its applicability to "open" learning situations consistent with many of the principles of lifelong education.

There are a variety of other qualitative approaches to inquiry, some of which are occasionally applied in contemporary evaluations. In *participant observation* the evaluator is by definition an internal agent. Everhart (1977) has recently written about the kinds of pressures towards assimilation into the value system of other participants that affect an evaluator in this role. Participant observation is being tried out in evaluation and more will be known about its usefulness in the relatively near future.

It is perhaps ideal to be able to study educational phenomena as they occur, but restricting evaluation to the contemporary leaves out much potentially valuable information. *Historical methods* may be the only way to learn about the effectiveness of many educational efforts. The relevance of educational biographies to the study of self-directed learning has already been cited. The recollections of participants, obtained through interviews or the study of documents and records, are essential tools in this type of research.

The above methods of inquiry, and others as well, deserve further exploration as evaluation tools for lifelong education. Unlike rigorous experimental methods, these approaches address the world as it is without contriving special conditions for research. They are also (with the exception of historical methods) readily adaptable to formative modes of evaluation and to the employment of internal evaluation agents.

One additional model of inquiry deserves special attention. This one is not so much a model for the acquisition of information as it is for the evaluation and arbitration of information coming from different sources.   It is derived not from science, but from jurisprudence, although the two approaches have obvious parallels as pointed out by Levine (1974).   Generally referred to as the *adversary model*, this method incorporates analogues for the rules by which evidence is admitted in the courtroom and by which different and often conflicting views of events are juxtaposed in reaching a legal decision.   Conflicting views about the value of educational endeavors among those who are affected are the norm rather than the exception. Learners, parents, teachers, curriculum developers, political figures, and others often have strikingly different perceptions of the worth of a given activity.   The objective information collected by evaluators under the experimental paradigm may be in conflict with the views of one or more of these groups.   The adversary model is designed to bring such views to the fore, to assess their basis in fact, and to reach the most sensible conclusion on the basis of that assessment.   This process clearly involves the exercise of judgment and the willingness to accept that Levine (1974) refers to as a "probabilistic decision criterion."   But it can also be argued that most social sciences also must make use of the same kind of criterion in arriving at conclusions.   Pertinent to the above discussion, Levine notes:

"It is necessary that the evidence be observable and
subject to criticism and rebuttal, but it is not necessary for it to be quantitative in nature, or for
the arguments to be restricted to those matters that
can be demonstrated on statistical grounds alone. It
is no argument against such a model that one cannot
generalize to populations, for in practice we do not
do that now. Moreover, the ties to the real world in
this model reside in the thoroughness with which we
are able to seek out and test evidence. The legal
model seems to provide flexibility in the types of

evidence with which we can deal. It also provides
for the ability of the human intelligence to select
relevant evidence, to weigh evidence, or to use evidence relativistically. From these viewpoints the
model holds promise of allowing us to deal rigorously with complex issues that now baffle us because we
rely exclusively on approaches ill-adapted to the active, social, historical human being." (p.674)

Levine has argued for the adversary model as an alternative
approach to arriving at conclusions in the social sciences. Its
relevance to evaluation is striking. This is especially the
case when evaluative data are open to the charge of subjectivity
by virtue of being collected by means of less formal methods of
inquiry. The adversary approach for evaluation genuinely merits
exploration and try out as a means for weighing evidence from
different sources and resolving differences in such evidence.

Conclusion

The three problem areas discussed in this final chapter
each refer to major areas of inquiry. They will not be resolved
easily nor without the involvement of many individuals. They
would be important to the development of evaluation practice
under any set of educational principles, but their special per-
tinence to lifelong education should be evident. If a better,
more effective, practice of evaluation is to be seen in the
future, one that does not often disrupt the educational practice to which it is applied, then these areas of inquiry must
be fully explored.

REFERENCES

Alkin, M.C. "Evaluation Theory Development", *Evaluation Comment*, Center for the Study of Evaluation, University of California, Los Angeles, 2(1969), No. 1, pp. 2-7.

Anderson, R.C. "How to construct achievement tests to assess comprehension", *Review of Educational Research*, 42(1972), pp. 145-170.

Arasian, P.W. "An application of a mastery learning stragegy", *Psychology in the Schools*, 9(1972), pp. 130-134.

Archambault, R.D. (ed.). *John Dewey on Education: Selected Writings*. Chicago: University of Chicago, 1974.

Averch, H.A. et al. *How Effective is Schooling? A Critical Review and Synthesis of Research Findings*. Santa Monica, Calif.: Rand, 1972.

Bennis, W.G. "The Case Study", *Journal of Applied Behavioral Science*, 4(1968), No. 2, pp. 227-231.

Berlyne, D.E. "Curiosity and Education", in *Learning and the Educational Process*, edited by J.D. Krumboltz. Chicago: Rand McNally, 1965, pp. 67-89.

Biggs, J.B. "Content to Process", *Australian Journal of Education*, 17(1973), pp. 225-238.

Block, J.H. "The effects of various levels of performance on selected cognitive, affective, and time variables." Unpublished Ph.D. dissertation, University of Chicago, 1970.

Block, J.R. "Operating principles for mastery learning", in *Mastery Learning: Theory and Practice*, edited by J.H. Block. New York: Holt, Rinehart, and Winston, 1971.

Bloom, B.S. *Taxonomy of Educational Objectives: Cognitive Domain*. New York: David McKay, 1956.

Bloom, B.S. "Learning for mastery", *Evaluation Comment*, 1(1968), No. 2.

Bloom, B.S. et al. *Handbook on Formative and Summative Evaluation of Student Learning*. New York: McGraw-Hill, 1971.

Bloom, B.S. "Mastery learning and its implications for curriculum development", in *Confronting Curriculum Reform*, edited by E.W. Eisner. Boston: Little Brown, 1971a.

Bloom, B.S. "Affective consequences of school achievement", in *Mastery Learning: Theory and Practice*, edited by J.H. Block. New York: Holt, Rinehart, and Winston, 1971b.

Bormuth, J.R. *On the Theory of Achievement Test Items*. Chicago: University of Chicago Press, 1970.

Carroll, J.B. "A Model of School Learning", *Teachers College Record*, 64(1963), pp. 723-733.

Carroll, J.B. "Problems of Measurement Related to the Concept of Learning for Mastery", in *Mastery Learning: Theory and Practice*, edited by J.H. Block. New York: Holt, Rinehart, and Winston, 1971.

Chein, I., Cook, S.W., and Harding, J. "The Field of Action Research", *The American Psychologist*, 1(1948), pp. 497-510.

Council of Europe, *Symposium on Factors in Primary and Secondary Education which Determine the Effectiveness of Further Education Later in Life*. Pont-à-Mousson, France, Jan. 11-17, 1972, (Report), p. 10.

Cronbach, L.J. "Course Improvement Through Evaluation", *Teachers College Record*, 64(1963), pp. 672-683.

Cronbach, L.J. "Validation of Educational Measures", *Proceedings of the 1969 Invitational Conference on Testing Problems*. Princeton: Educational Testing Service, 1969.

Cronbach, L.J. "Comments on Mastery Learning and its Implications for Curriculum Development", in *Confronting Curriculum Reform*, edited by E.W. Eisner. Boston: Little, Brown, 1971a, pp. 49-55.

Cronbach, L.J. "Test Validation", in *Educational Measurement*, edited by R.L. Thorndike. Washington, D.C.: American Council on Education, 1971b, pp. 443-507.

Cronbach, L.J. "Beyond the two disciplines of scientific psychology", *American Psychologist*, 30(1975), pp. 116-127.

Cross, K.P. "The Elusive Goal of Educational Equality", *Adult Leadership*, 28(1975), No. 8, pp. 227-232.

Dahllof, U. *Date on curriculum and teaching process: Do they make any difference to non-significant test differences - And under what conditions?* University of Göteborg, Sweden: Institute of Education, Publication No. 30, 1973.

Dave, R.H. *Lifelong Education and School Curriculum.* UIE Monographs 1. Hamburg: Unesco Institute for Education, 1973, pp. 90.

Dave, R.H., (ed.). *Reflections on Lifelong Education and the School.* UIE Monographs 3. Hamburg: Unesco Institute for Education, 1975.

Dave, R.H. and Legrand, P. "De l'enseignement à l'apprentissage", *International Review of Education*, 20(1974), No. 4, pp. 447-461.

Dave, R.H. and Stiemerling, N. *Lifelong Education and the School: Abstracts and Bibliography.* UIE Monographs 2. Hamburg: Unesco Institute for Education, 1973.

Ebel, R.L. "Criterion-referenced measurements: Limitations", *School Review*, 79(1971), pp. 282-297.

Eisner, E.W. "Instructional and Expressive Educational Objectives: Their Formulation and Use in Curriculum", in *Instructional Objectives*, AERA Series on Curriculum Evaluation, No. 3, by W.J. Popham et al. Chicago: Rand McNally, 1968, pp. 1-18.

Evans, J.W. and Williams, W. "The Politics of Evaluation: The Case of Head Start", in *Evaluating Social Programs*, edited by P.H. Rossi and W. Williams. New York: Seminar Press, 1972, pp. 247-264.

Everhart, R.B. "Between Stranger and Friend: Some Consequences of 'Long Term' Fieldwork in Schools", *American Educational Research Journal*, 14(1977), pp. 1-15.

Faure, Edgar. *Learning to Be, the World of Education Today and Tomorrow.* Paris: Unesco, 1972.

Fenstermacher, G.D. "Satisfaction: An Alternative Criterion for School Success", in *The Conventional and the Alternative in Education*, by J.I. Goodlad et al. Berkeley, Calif.: McCutchan, 1975, pp. 215-240.

Flanagan, J.C. "Functional education for the seventies", *Phi Delta Kappan*, 49(1967), pp. 27-32.

Flanagan, J.C. "Program for learning in accordance with needs", *Psychology in the Schools*, 6(1969), pp. 133-136.

Fredriksson, L. and Gestrelius, K. "Lifelong Learning in Swedish Curricula", *Didakometry No. 48*, University of Malmö, School of Education, (1975).

Gagné, R.M. "The Implications of Instructional Objectives for Learning", in *Defining Educational Objectives*, by C.M. Lindvall. Pittsburg: University of Pittsburg Press, 1964, pp. 37-46.

Gagné, R.M. *Conditions of Learning.* New York: Holt, Rinehart, and Winston, 1965.

Glaser, R. "Adapting the Elementary School Curriculum to Individual Performance", in *Proceedings of the 1967 Invitational Conference on Testing Problems.* Princeton: Educational Testing Service, 1968.

Glaser, R., and Nitko, A.J. "Measurement in Learning and Instruction", in *Educational Measurement* (2nd ed.), edited by R.L. Thorndike. Washington: American Council on Education, 1971.

Goodlad, J.I. with Richter, M., Jr. *The Development of a Conceptual System for Dealing with Problems of Curriculum and Instruction.* Los Angeles, Calif.: University of California, Los Angeles, 1966.

Goodlad, J.I. "A Typology of Educational Alternatives", in *The Conventional and the Alternative in Education*, by J.I.

Goodlad. Berkeley, Calif.: McCutchan, 1975.

Guilford, J.P. *The Nature of Human Intelligence*. New York:
McGraw-Hill, 1967.

Hambleton, R.K. "Testing and decision-making procedures for
selected individualized instructional programs", *Review of
Educational Research*, 44(1974), pp. 371-400.

Hargreaves, D.H. "Deschoolers and New Romantics", in *Educability, Schools, and Ideology*, by M. Flude and J. Ahier. London:
Croom Helm, 1974, pp. 186-210.

Harris, C.W. "Some technical characteristics of mastery tests",
in *Problems in Criterion-referenced Measurement*, CSE Monograph Series in Evaluation (3), edited by C.W. Harris, M.C.
Alkin and W.J. Popham. Los Angeles: Center for the Study of
Evaluation, University of California, Los Angeles, 1974.

Havelock, R. *Planning for Innovation Through Dissemination and
Utilization*. Ann Arbor, Michigan: University of Michigan,
1971.

Heath, R.W. "Curriculum Evaluation", in *Encyclopedia of Educational Research*, 4th Ed., edited by R.L. Ebel. New York:
MacMillan, 1969, pp. 280-283.

Hively, W. et al. *Domain-referenced Curriculum Evaluation: A
Technical Handbook and a Case Study from the MINNEMAST Pro-
ject*. CSE Monograph Series in Evaluation (1), Los Angeles:
Center for the Study of Evaluation, University of California,
Los Angeles, 1973.

Holt, J. *Freedom and Beyond*. New York: E.P. Dutton, 1972.

Huberman, A.M. *Understanding Change in Education: An Introduction*. Experiments and Innovations in Education, No. 4.
Paris: Unesco, IBE, 1973.

Husén, T. "Lifelong Learning in the Educative Society", *Con-
vergence*, 1(1968), No. 4, pp. 12-21.

Illich, I.D. *Deschooling Society*. New York: Harper & Row,
1971.

Joyce, B. and Weil, M. *Models of Teaching*. Englewood Cliffs,

New Jersey: Prentice-Hall, 1972.

Kim, Y. et al. *An Application of a New Instructional Model.* Korean Educational Development Institute, Research Report No. 8, 1974.

La Belle, T.J. and Verhine, R.E. "Nonformal Education and Oc- cupational Stratification: Implications for Latin America", *Harvard Educational Review,* 45(1975), No. 2, pp. 160-190.

Lebouteux, F. "The School in an Age of Continuous Education", *Education and Culture,* 21(1973), pp. 8-14.

Lengrand, P. *An Introduction to Lifelong Education.* Paris: Unesco, 1970.

Levine, M. "Scientific Method and the Adversary Model: Some Preliminary Thoughts", *American Psychologist,* 29(1974), No. 9, pp. 661-677.

Lewis, C., Wang, M., and Novick, M.R. "Marginal Distributions for the Estimation of Proportions in *m* Groups", *The Technical Bulletin, No. 13.* Iowa City: American College Testing Pro- gram, 1973.

Macdonald, J.B. "An Evaluation of Evaluation", *Urban Review,* 7(1974), No. 1, pp. 3-14.

McClelland, D.C. "Testing for competence rather than for intel- ligence", *American Psychologist,* 28(1973), pp. 1-12.

Maher, M.L. and Stallings, W.M. "Freedom from External Evalua- tion", *Child Development,* 43(1972), pp. 177-185.

March, J.A. "Model Bias in Social Action", *Review of Educa- tional Research,* 42(1972), No. 4, pp. 413-429.

Maslow, A. *Motivation and Personality.* New York: Harper, 1954.

Millman, J. "Passing scores and test lengths for domain-ref- erenced tests", *Review of Educational Research,* 43(1973), pp. 205-216.

Millman, J. "Criterion-referenced measurement", in *Evaluation in Education: Current Applications,* edited by W.J. Popham. Berkeley: McCutchan, 1974.

Moore, O.K. *Autotelic Response Environments in Exceptional Children.* Hamden, Conn.: Responsive Environments, 1963.

Morrison, H.C. *The Practice of Teaching in the Secondary School.* Chicago: University of Chicago Press, 1926.

Novick, M.R. and Lewis, C. *Prescribing Test Length for Criterion-referenced Measurement.* CSE Monograph Series in Evaluation (3). Los Angeles: Center for the Study of Evaluation, University of California, Los Angeles, 1974.

Parkyn, G.W. *Towards a Conceptual Model of Lifelong Education.* Paris: Unesco, 1973.

Payne, D.A. *Curriculum Evaluation.* Lexington, Massachusetts: D.C. Heath, 1974.

Popham, W.J. *Educational evaluation.* Englewood Cliffs, New Jersey: Prentice-Hall, 1977.

Postman, N. and Weingartner, C. *Teaching as a Subversive Activity.* New York: Delacorte Press, 1969.

Provus, M. *Discrepancy Evaluation: For Educational Program Improvement and Assessment.* Berkeley, California: McCutchan, 1971.

Richmond, W.K. *Education and Schooling.* London: Methuen, 1975.

Rogers, C.R. *Freedom to Learn.* Columbus, Ohio: Charles E. Merrill, 1969.

Sax, G. "The use of standardized tests in evaluation", in *Evaluation in Education,* edited by W.J. Popham. Berkeley, Calif.: McCutchan, 1974, pp. 245-308.

Schwartz, B. "A Prospective View of Permanent Education", in *A Compendium of Studies Commissioned by the Council for Cultural Cooperation.* Strasbourg: Council of Europe, 1970.

Schwartz, B. "A Prospective View of Permanent Education", in *Permanent Education.* Strasbourg: Council of Europe, 1970.

Scriven, M. "The Methodology of Evaluation", in *Perspectives of Curriculum Evaluation,* AERA Monograph Series No. 1. Chicago: Rand McNally, 1967.

Scriven, M. "Pros and Cons About Goal-Free Evaluation", *Evaluation Comment*. Center for the Study of Evaluation, University of California, Los Angeles, 2(1972), No. 4, pp. 1-4.

Shavelson, R.J., Beckum, L.C. and Brown, B. "A criterion sampling approach to selecting patrolmen", *The Police Chief*, September 1974, pp. 55-61.

Shavelson, R.J., Hubner, J.J., and Stanton, G.C. "Self-Concept: Validation of Construc\` \`nterpretations", *Review of Educational Research*, 46(1´), pp. 407-441.

Shoemaker, D.M. "Toward a framework for achievement testing", *Review of Educational Research*, 45(1975), pp. 127-148.

Skager, R.W. "The system for objectives-based evaluation--reading", *Evaluation Comment*, Center for the Study of Evaluation, University of California, Los Angeles, 3(1971), No. 1, pp. 6-11.

Skager, R.W. and Dave, R.H. *Curriculum Evaluation for Lifelong Education*. Oxford: Pergamon, 1977.

Spady, W.G. "Competency Based Education: A Bandwagon in Search of a Definition", *Educational Researcher*, 6(1977), No. 1, pp. 9-14.

Spaulding, S. "Life-Long Education: A Modest Model for Planning and Research", *Comparative Education*, 10(1974), pp. 101-113.

Stake, R.E. "School Accountability Laws", *Evaluation Comment*. Center for the Study of Evaluation, University of California, Los Angeles, 4(1973), No. 1, pp. 1-3.

Stodolsky, S.S. "Identifying and Evaluating Open Education", *Phi Delta Kappan*, 57 (1975), No. 2, pp. 113-117.

Stufflebeam, D.L. *Evaluation as Enlightenment for Decision-Making*. Columbus, Ohio: Evaluation Center, Ohio State University, 1968.

Suchman, J.R. "A Model for the Analysis of Inquiry", in *Analyses of Concept Learning*, edited by H.J. Klausmeier and C.W. Harris. New York: Academic Press, 1966, pp. 177-187.

Suchodolski, B. *Trzy Pedagogiki* (A Third Pedagogy). Warsaw:

Nasza Ksiegarnia, 1970.

Tough, A. *The Adult's Learning Projects*. Ontario: The Ontario Institute for Studies in Education, Research in Education Series No. 1, 1971.

Washburn, C.W. "Educational Measurements as a Key to Individualizing Instruction and Promotions", *Journal of Educational Research*, 5(1922), pp. 195-206.

Weinburg, C. and Skager R.W. "The Relation Between Processes and Values: An Alternative Function for Evaluation", in *The Conventional and the Alternative in Education*, by J.I. Goodlad et al. Berkeley, Calif.: McCutchan, 1975.

Wilson, H.A. "A Judgmental Approach to Criterion-Referenced Testing", in *Problems in Criterion-Referenced Measurement*, edited by C.W. Harris, M.C. Alkin, and W.J. Popham. Center for the Study of Evaluation, University of California, Los Angeles, 1974.

Worthen, B.R. and Sanders, J.R. *Educational Evaluation: Theory and Practice*. Worthington, Ohio: Charles A. Jones, 1973.

Wroczyñski, R. "Learning Styles and Lifelong Education", *International Review of Education*, 20(1974), No. 4, pp. 464-473.

INDEX